TRIALS
AND
TRIUMPHS

Hope Beyond Circumstances:
Forty Life-Changing Testimonies

FAITHWRITERS

MINDSTIR MEDIA

Published by Mindstir Media
1931 Woodbury Ave. #182 | Portsmouth, NH 03801 | USA
1.800.767.0531 | www.mindstirmedia.com

Printed in the United States of America
ISBN-13: 978-0-9914884-0-7

ACKNOWLEDGEMENTS

The idea for this book was birthed by the notable perseverance in the faith, despite great struggles, of two of our best staff members (Amy Michelle Wiley and Shann Hall-LochmannVanBennekom), along with many in our general membership who are an inspiration to us all.

FaithWriters wishes to acknowledge and thank all of our members who submitted their honest, heartfelt testimonies to be considered for this book.   Everyone who submitted a testimony showed openness, honesty, and sincere desire to see the lost come to Christ; this truly humbles us. Your willingness to come out into the light and share with the world is refreshing. Your lives are a living testimony. We thank everyone greatly for your support and membership.

We would also like to thank all of the members who helped to make this book possible. Thank you to our judges (Lynda Schab, Marie Grosset, Nicole Wian, Karen Maloy and Nicole Anderson) who despite very busy schedules volunteered and diligently read all of the submissions, making the hard choices.

Thank you to our editors (Amy Michelle Wiley, Shann Hall-LochmannVanBennekom, and Teresa Crumpton) who worked patiently with forty authors.

Thank you to Paula Titus for crafting the prologue and epilogue in a powerful way.

Thank you to J.J. Hebert and MindStir Media for working with us to bring this book to publication.

Michael & Bea Edwards
FaithWriters.com

HOPE BEYOND CIRCUMSTANCES

The Bible is filled with HOPE as the following verses indicate. These verses were taken from the English Standard Version (ESV) of the Holy Bible.

• For God so loved the world, that he gave his only Son, that whoever believes in him should not perish but have eternal life. John 3:16

• Whoever believes in him is not condemned, but whoever does not believe is condemned already, because he has not believed in the name of the only Son of God. John 3:18

• Now faith is the assurance of things hoped for, the conviction of things not seen. Hebrews 11:1

• Let us hold fast the confession of our hope without wavering, for he who promised is faithful. Romans 8:1

• There is therefore now no condemnation for those who are in Christ Jesus. Hebrews 10:23

• For in this hope we were saved. Now hope that is seen is not hope. For who hopes for what he sees? But if we hope for what we do not see, we wait for it with patience. Romans 8:24-25

• Rejoice in hope, be patient in tribulation, be constant in prayer. Romans 12:12

• So when God desired to show more convincingly to the heirs of the promise the unchangeable character of his purpose, he guaranteed it with an oath, so that by two unchangeable things, in which it is impossible for God to lie, we who have fled for refuge might have strong encouragement to hold fast to the hope set before us. We have this as a sure and steadfast anchor of the soul, a hope that enters into the inner place behind the curtain, where Jesus has gone as a forerunner on our behalf, having become a high priest forever after the order of Melchizedek. Hebrews 6:17-20

• For whatever was written in former days was written for our instruction, that through endurance and through the encouragement of the Scriptures we might have hope. Romans 15:4

• May the God of hope fill you with all joy and peace in believing, so that by the power of the Holy Spirit you may abound in hope. Romans 15:13

• God is not man, that he should lie, or a son of man, that he should change his mind. Has he said, and will he not do it? Or has he spoken, and will he not fulfill it? Numbers 23:19

• Though he slay me, I will hope in him; yet I will argue my ways to his face. Job 13:15

• For I know the plans I have for you, declares the LORD, plans for welfare and not for evil, to give you a future and a hope. Jeremiah 29:11

• When the cares of my heart are many, your consolations cheer my soul. Psalm 94:19

• But they who wait for the LORD shall renew their strength; they shall mount up with wings like eagles; they shall run and not be weary; they shall walk and not faint. Isaiah 40:31

• When you pass through the waters, I will be with you; and through the rivers, they shall not overwhelm you; when you walk through fire you shall not be burned, and the flame shall not consume you. Isaiah 43:2

- The steadfast love of the LORD never ceases; his mercies never come to an end; they are new every morning; great is your faithfulness. "The LORD is my portion," says my soul, "therefore I will hope in him." Lamentations 3:22-24

- And we know that for those who love God all things work together for good, for those who are called according to his purpose. Romans 8:28

- May the God of hope fill you with all joy and peace in believing, so that by the power of the Holy Spirit you may abound in hope. Romans 15:13

- So we do not lose heart. Though our outer self is wasting away, our inner self is being renewed day by day. For this light momentary affliction is preparing for us an eternal weight of glory beyond all comparison, as we look not to the things that are seen but to the things that are unseen. For the things that are seen are transient, but the things that are unseen are eternal. 2 Corinthians 4:16-18

- Therefore, if anyone is in Christ, he is a new creation. The old has passed away; behold, the new has come. 2 Corinthians 5:17

- Now to him who is able to do far more abundantly than all that we ask or think, according to the power at work within us, to him be glory in the church and in Christ Jesus throughout all generations, forever and ever. Amen. Ephesians 3:20-21

- Brothers, I do not consider that I have made it my own. But one thing I do: forgetting what lies behind and straining forward to what lies ahead, I press on toward the goal for the prize of the upward call of God in Christ Jesus. Philippians 3:13-14

- But since we belong to the day, let us be sober, having put on the breastplate of faith and love, and for a helmet the hope of salvation. 1 Thessalonians 5:8

- But God shows his love for us in that while we were still sinners, Christ died for us. Romans 5:8

- Now may our Lord Jesus Christ himself, and God our Father, who loved us and gave us eternal comfort and good hope through grace, comfort your hearts and establish them in every good work and word. 2 Thessalonians 2:16–17

- Blessed be the God and Father of our Lord Jesus Christ! According to his great mercy, he has caused us to be born again to a living hope through the resurrection of Jesus Christ from the dead. 1 Peter 1:3

- So that by two unchangeable things, in which it is impossible for God to lie, we who have fled for refuge might have strong encouragement to hold fast to the hope set before us. We have this as a sure and steadfast anchor of the soul, a hope that enters into the inner place behind the curtain Hebrews 6:18-19

- Now faith is the assurance of things hoped for, the conviction of things not seen. Hebrews 11:1

- He will wipe away every tear from their eyes, and death shall be no more, neither shall there be mourning, nor crying, nor pain anymore, for the former things have passed away." Revelation 21:4

- Do not be anxious about anything, but in everything by prayer and supplication with thanksgiving let your requests be made known to God. And the peace of God, which surpasses all understanding, will guard your hearts and your minds in Christ Jesus. Philippians 4:6-7

CONTENTS

ACKNOWLEDGEMENTS

HOPE BEYOND CIRCUMSTANCES

TABLE OF CONTENTS

PROLOGUE   1

COMING TO FAITH

A LIFE OF REDEMPTION   5
By Paul Holway

AN EFFECTIVE FERVENT PRAYER   9
By Sandra Fischer

DARKNESS TO LIGHT,   13
REVELATION TO REDEMPTION
By Rad Khan

DISILLUSIONMENT   17
TO DELIGHT
By Dave Walker

FINDING PEACE   22
By Matthew Guddat

FROM DARE TO ETERNITY   26
By Dannie Hawley

FROM SLAVERY TO FREEDOM   30
By Kathleen Trissel

FROM SUICIDE TO SINGING   34
By Rick L. King

GOING THE DISTANCE   38
By Ennis Smith

HEARING GOD'S GENTLE VOICE   43
By Donna Mae Carrico

INFECTION OF EVIL   47
By Lynn Gipson

OUT OF THE SHADOWS   50
By Dorci Harris

THE OFFER   54
By Rachel Malcolm

THE PROMISE   58
By Lorraine Quirke

UNCLENCHING MY FIST   62
By Leigh Ann Reid

UNEXPECTED   66
By Joanne Sher

FAITH UNDER FIRE

A TRIPLE DOSE OF GRACE   73
By Chris Goglin

ACCEPTING SUFFERING FROM HIS HAND   78
By Andrea Van Ye

BROKEN-HEARTED WHOLENESS   82
By Frankie Kemp

BUILT ON THE ROCK   86
By JoAnne E. Billison

CHRISTMAS ANGELS   90
By Leola Ogle

EXCEPT GOD 94
By Allison Egley

FROM FAILURE TO FAITH 98
By Barbara Caldwell

"I'M NOT SHAKING; 101
I'M LIVING IN PEACE"
By Sheila L. Mills

GOD BELIEVES IN ME? 105
By Shann Hall-LochmannVanBennekom

GOD'S VIEW 109
IS BETTER THAN OURS
By Sally Stap

I AM NOT ALONE 113
By Amber Leggette-Aldrich

MY 9/11 117
By Ken Ebright

MY JERICHO WALL 120
By Amy Michelle Wiley

MY LIFEBOAT 124
By K.D. Manes

MY NAME IS ON HIS HAND 128
By Allison Reed

NEVER GIVE UP... 133
ALWAYS LET GO
By Phyllis Stokes

THE BLESSING 137
By Phee Paradise

THE HEALING HAND   140
OF PERFECT GRACE
By Melissa Doerksen

THE ARGUMENT   145
By Laura Hawbaker

UNRAVELED   148
By Mimi Marie

WHY IS HE DOING THIS   152
TO ME NOW?
By Lori Dixon

A TESTIMONY THAT INSPIRED ME

A MAN CALLED HARRY   159
By Jim Oates

A TIME BOMB IN MY TUMMY   163
ANNE'S STORY
By Luella Campbell

HE CAME TO STAY IN MY HEART   167
By Pauline Brakebill

EPILOGUE   170
INVITATION TO ACCEPT JESUS   173

PROLOGUE

All of us experience painful moments in life. Sometimes those moments turn into days, months, and even years. There are losses of all kinds—by death, divorce, betrayal, or maybe the loss of a job, health, or possessions. Maybe your loss has been inward, with loss of peace, joy, or contentment. Christians struggle with these same issues, and if you aren't a Christian you may question this reality. Why do these Christians continually rely on this thing called faith; where is their God, and what's the point?

If you are struggling with the pain of life, this book will comfort you because you are not alone. You may even realize you're much better off than you thought. These pages will reveal precisely why these Bible-believing followers of Christ cling to their faith in spite of loss, devastation, and disappointments. Our plea is that you will honestly consider the stories in this book and give inspection to this Savior called Jesus.

Forty true stories lie naked on the pages of this book like an open wound, pounding and pulsing to the rhythm of forty heartbeats. The words themselves may bleed and spill over with each turn of the page. Though limbs have been severed, lives have been changed, all to the glory of the King of Kings, Jesus Christ.

When God told Noah He was going to make it rain for forty days and forty nights, Noah didn't build the ark with comfort in mind. Noah's goal was to be confident it would weather the storm. Nor did the forty people, who tell their stories in this book, have comfort in mind when they built their lives around Christ. This is exactly why they, like Noah, keep their faith in spite of torrential downpours. Jesus doesn't remove the disturbances; He is the shelter in the meanwhile.

Manna, the bread that fell from the sky which fed the Israelites for forty years, was their sustenance. This heavenly food nourished them, sustained them, and kept them alive. Yet in the pages of

1

Scripture, it's not long before the Israelites began complaining about the manna and wanted something different. They were bored—it no longer satisfied. Jesus said, "I am the bread of life that comes down from Heaven."

The Christians in this book will explain why Jesus, the "Living Bread," never loses the ability to satisfy. Food appeases hunger only temporarily because it doesn't have the power to permanently compensate for what is lacking, so we must come to the table, again and again. But Jesus, He is sufficient to atone for every need—even life—permanently, completely, and delightfully.

The folks at FaithWriters pray that everyone who reads this book will be encouraged and that Christians will be reminded that the Savior Jesus Christ will carry us through our storms, whether they last for forty days or forty years. When the troubles of this world seek to choke our faith and starve our affections, let us remember the faithful ones in this book, who, because they continued to feast on Him, the Bread of Life, were filled with hope and perseverance. Never giving up, they march on toward that great reward of eternal life with Christ.

This book is also for nonbelievers. We pray that you will to come to realize your need for the Savior Jesus Christ. Don't choose Him as a way to avoid the storms of life, because they will come. Noah's ark provided a way to escape death, not a way to escape the storm. Come to Christ because you recognize your need for a Savior to save you from eternal death. *"For God so loved the world, that He gave His only son, that whoever believes in Him should not perish but have eternal life." (John 3:16 ESV)*

Paula Titus

TRIALS AND TRIUMPHS
COMING TO FAITH

A LIFE OF REDEMPTION

By Paul Holway

I had what on the outside looked like a normal childhood—two parents at home, an older brother, a younger sister, and my dad was very involved at church. He was devoted to God, but we didn't have a strong relationship. As the middle child, I felt left out.

My mom was the disciplinarian. She had a bad temper; she inspired fear; she left bruises on me.

Although the family looked like we "had it all together," inside, I was crying out for help. I got into trouble and I got bullied in school and I turned everything inward—all the hurt, anger, and frustrations of never being able to defend myself. I stuffed all those feelings inside.

As a child, my way of feeling any power or control was to abuse animals who couldn't defend themselves any more than I could.

Full of rage, I cursed God because I felt like he'd divided our family. I hated Him for taking my dad away. When he wasn't at work, he was at church and not home with us.

I started to hate myself, and I thought of ways to kill myself, but God had His hand on me the entire time. He put enough fear of death in me that I never attempted suicide.

When I turned twelve, I became so cold inside that I saw people as objects. One day I had been in trouble at school. On the bus ride home, I thought about any way possible to avoid the punishment I had coming. I was so scared I thought about running away, but I had nowhere to go.

In my blind hatred, my bizarre decision was to shoot my eight-year-old sister so my mom wouldn't dare touch me again. She'd be scared of me for a change! I loaded my dad's hunting rifle and went into my sister's room. She didn't even see the gun, but I pulled the trigger and shot her. She died on the way to the hospital.

I was sentenced to juvenile life (five years), where my heart hardened even more, and my hate for life grew. But my parents and our church never stopped praying for me and my family.

Even in confinement, God was there with me. One day, a woman showed up to visit me. I had never seen her before, but she gave me a Bible and prayed with me.

Filled with pain, grief, and hatred, I began to hurt myself by hitting walls and making eraser burns on my hands and arms. When I punished myself, I felt better temporarily. I deserved to hurt.

Still God never left me. He continually had people I didn't know visit me and share their faith. When I was sixteen, I had one year left to serve. If God was into clichés, He'd say I was a tough nut to crack. When I was released, my plan was to become a biker, hang out in bars, and get into fights.

But a group of bikers (Christian Motorcyclist Association) came to the jail once a month for Bible studies. God used these men and women to continue watering that seed He had planted in spite of my juvenile and destructive plans.

Once I got out, I moved back into the house where I had killed my sister and started twelfth grade. It was a difficult transition, to say the least. I didn't belong there with my parents; I didn't know them as my parents.

I got hooked up with some of my old friends and started drinking and smoking weed with them. They accepted me. I started taking speed at the same time I was getting high so I wouldn't crash, and the next day I'd wake up with my heart pounding in my chest like it was going to explode. I continued to cut my arms with knives and burn myself with lighters. I still needed to be punished. I cut my left wrist deep enough that I cut the nerve and tendon and lost all feeling in two fingers.

Even though my life was drenched in sin, God continued to protect me. But at the time, I couldn't see it.

One day from a hotel room where I worked, I stole a pistol—a felony charge. The district attorney wanted to throw me in prison. But by the grace of God, I got three years' probation, and God finally broke through. He led me to make a change. I left town and moved in with a woman who is now my wife.

I started to get off drugs. For a while, I still smoked weed and drank, but I quit using speed. I worked with a woman—she and her husband were both bikers—and I soon found out they were Christians.

The woman invited me to church one night, and I knew I had to go. By that time, I was married, but my wife didn't want to go. So I went to the church alone.

As the pastor was saying the closing prayer, this rush of emotion just hit me! All the feelings I'd held in for so long, the people I'd hurt, the lives I'd messed up—all of it surfaced. I got up to leave, and my friend stopped me. I just started crying and couldn't stop.

The pastor came over, and I confessed to him that I had killed my little sister. He led me in a prayer that has changed my life forever: I gave my life to Jesus that night. I was forgiven. When I felt God wrap His arms around me that first time, I finally knew, this was what true unconditional love was. My life had been redeemed.

Now, fifteen years later, I am drug-free and, even though I'd cut my tendon and nerve, I'm playing the guitar the best I've ever played and getting better. I currently play lead guitar on our worship team at church praising God.

Our marriage is healed and getting stronger. We have a ten-year-old son, who is growing up to know the Lord. My wife and son are truly gifts from God.

God took a broken, beat-down soul with no purpose or reason to go on and gave me the love that I so desperately needed. He gave me life, a purpose, and a reason to go on.

When God got a hold of my heart, as painful and hard as it was, I began to be transformed into a child of the King! He showed me how to love by the love He gave me.

The enemy doesn't want healing for any of us, but God does.

Yes, I'm a murderer, a liar, a thief, an adulterer. I've had idols before God, cursed His name, and degraded my parents, but God has the victory.

Jesus died on the cross for my sins, and now I stand spotless before my King. Satan has no authority or power to take that from me.

Jesus has forgiven me for all of my sin and is my guarantee of spending eternity in heaven praising my heavenly Father. And I will be reunited with my sister.

I pray that whoever reads my story will realize that no matter how messed up our lives may be, there is hope. It doesn't matter how many crimes we've committed or how many people we've hurt, Jesus loves us unconditionally.

He died so we can have eternal life, and there is no better sacrifice than that. We need to ask for forgiveness of our sin, believe in our hearts that Jesus died and God raised Him from the dead, and acknowledge Jesus as our Lord and Savior.

Your life will never be the same!

ABOUT THE AUTHOR

Paul Holway is a member of Christ Life Church and serves on the worship team, playing lead guitar and bass guitar. He loves outdoors activities like hiking, camping, and fishing. Paul is also the owner and photographer of Holway Images. Paul presently resides in Casa Grande, Arizona, USA with his beautiful wife and son.

You can learn more about this author at:
http://faithwriters.com/testimonies.php

An Effective Fervent Prayer

By Sandra Fischer

How long would you pray for someone to receive the saving grace of Christ? A year? If you're diligent, maybe two or even three? How about fifteen years? That's the number of years my friend Marlene prayed for a friend of hers who, although she declared herself to be a believer, displayed no real fruit of being a Christian.

Marlene's friend gave the appearance of having a happy life, but her heart harbored misery. She had all the trappings of what others might deem as enviable—a college degree, marriage to a successful businessman, three healthy daughters, a beautiful lakefront home, and membership in all the elite social groups in the community. Yet—beneath the veneer of a "happily-ever-after" picture lay a bleak void in her life.

As long as everyone lived up to her expectations or if things went her way, she was pleased. If not, she would explode in anger or pout for days. If she planned on dinner out, and her tired husband came home and insisted they stay in to eat, she would mope for days. If one of her daughters didn't obey her demands for perfection, she railed at her.

One of her fits of anger erupted during an evening meal when one of her daughters misbehaved. As she stormed about, throwing utensils and spitting fuming words like fiery darts, her nine-year-old daughter ran from the table to her room. The mother ensued, bellowing the question of why she had left when her displeasure had not been levied toward her but to her sister. Amid tears, came the answer, "I don't want to see the kind of mother I will be when I

9

grow up!" Such insight caused introspection, but not enough to convict the woman to repent of her sinful ways.

Instead, she continued to believe that if others, particularly her husband and children, would simply do what she wanted, then life would be perfect, and she would have no need to react in volatile ways. She manipulated, she accused, she cajoled, hoping to convince everyone to serve her wishes. When they refused, she became increasingly bitter and made life dismal for everyone.

Her appearance as a believer in Christ was a façade as well. She was baptized as a teenager, but for all practical purposes it seemed it had been nothing more than an attempt to have "hell-fire insurance." She attended church regularly and even taught Sunday school, although she had never read or truly studied the Bible. She had no idea what a disservice her "cafeteria-style" teaching was to God and to her students—choosing to endorse scriptural principles she agreed with and minimizing or trying to discredit those she disliked.

Marlene knew her friend needed a personal relationship with Christ, so she continued to pray for her, to love her, and to spend time with her. Year after year, Marlene invited her to join in Bible studies or attend women's retreats, yet year after year she refused. But Marlene believed God and His promise to answer her fervent prayer, so she kept praying for her friend's heart to be softened toward the Lord.

After fifteen long years of praying, her friend's world came crashing down around her. Her marriage was in shambles, her children rebellious, and she was blinded by her pride. She could not see her role and responsibility in contributing to the misery in her life and the lives of others. She was in a deep pit and Marlene saw the situation as an opportunity for God to work. She believed God had allowed her friend's life to spiral downward to a place of brokenness—a place where she might open her heart to hear the Gospel. Marlene asked again if her friend would go with her to an upcoming retreat, and this time she assented.

The retreat was entitled "Lord, Change Me," and the main speaker was Evelyn Christenson, author of the book by the same title. God's providence was abundantly clear and working—her message was custom-designed for Marlene's friend, who believed in everyone else's need to repent while denying her own. During the retreat, she saw who needed to change and Who was the One to change her. She realized her need to admit her life was bankrupt because of her sin and how Christ was offering her the riches of both forgiveness and salvation. On the last day of the retreat, tears of gratitude fell as Marlene saw her prayers answered. Her friend received Christ's gift of grace and asked the Lord to change her.

He began a marvelous work in her that day as she trusted in Him, and to this very day, He is faithfully completing what He promised. I know, because I am that woman—I am Marlene's friend. How grateful I am to her for her faithful prayers and how thankful I am to both her and God for their unrelenting love—a love that would not let me go.

On that eventful day, I bought a new Bible and voraciously began to read it. I was so hungry for the spiritual food I had denied myself. I began to grow and change. I was blessed to get "into the Word" and am continually nourished by the Word getting "into me." I believe Paul spoke of me when he wrote, *"And I am sure of this, that He who began a good work in you will bring it to completion at the day of Jesus Christ." (Philippians1:6, ESV)* He is still changing me, patiently and lovingly.

I have garnered firsthand the truth of God's promise *". . .that for those who love God all things work together for good, for those who are called according to His purpose." (Romans 8:28, ESV)* I know more than ever His purpose to conform me to the image of Christ.

This truth has been manifested over and again in my life as the result of God answering the prayer of my faithful friend many years ago. Through His faithfulness, I have continued to study the Bible, to share my testimony, to disciple others, and to rest in His care. I have been blessed with many evidences of God's love, not the least of which is His healing my relationship with my husband. We celebrated our golden anniversary last year. He has blessed our children and grandchildren, and most of them have accepted Christ.

And now what do I pray? I pray just as dear Marlene prayed so fervently and effectively for me. I pray those who do not know Christ as Savior and Lord will believe and receive His gift of grace. I trust His providence no matter how long it may take—fifteen years or even more.

ABOUT THE AUTHOR

Sandra Fischer taught high school English and owned a Christian bookstore in Indiana for several years. Much of her writing is devoted to stories from her experiences growing up in the Midwest. She has been published in *Guideposts*, several anthologies and online in *Faithwriters Magazine*. Sandra is retired and lives in South Carolina with her husband, Craig. She is a platinum member of Faithwriters.com

To see more of her work, go to:
http://faithwriters.com/testimonies.php

DARKNESS TO LIGHT, REVELATION TO REDEMPTION

By Rad Khan

My conversion from Islam to Christianity is not as dramatic as some other converts. However, I was a sinner in need of a saviour. It is difficult for anyone to comprehend this fact, regardless of faith in anyone else but in Jesus Christ. My life in darkness was translated into life in the light, according to Matthew 4:6. The seed for my faith in Christ started in the country of birth, Guyana; it was, and still is, a country with people of different beliefs and faiths. Christianity was the predominant religion in that day, but there were other major world religions being practiced.

My parents followed some of Islam's religious practices in our home, but were not very involved in religion. My father attended the mosque on their 'high holy' days, and sometimes on a weekly basis. My brother and I were expected to attend as we got older; it was not an expectation of my sisters, but they were involved in many services or prayers in our home. However, it was just a ritual to me. I remember going to the mosque on many an occasion, and bowing down to pray to Mohammed with the rest of the followers. The people seemed to be genuinely devoted in their worship and beliefs. I cannot recall why I started to attend the mosque on a more regular basis, possibly, at the request of my father. The goal was to learn Urdu in order to read the Koran.

The teachings of the Imam were similar to going to school to learn any other subject, and I treated it as such, as I could find no life or revelation through it. I was beginning to grasp the language of the Koran, and we had to perform recitals by memory. It was during one such recital, that I left the mosque and only ever returned on their 'holy' days. I was around fourteen years of age and I could not recite one of the prayers, at that time, public discipline was still in effect in schools, but I never expected it in the mosque. The Imam told me to hold out my hand to receive my punishment. The bamboo whip missed my hand and split my wrist, and it started to bleed. The Imam was going to hit me again, but I grabbed the cane, broke it and threw it at him—I remember telling him, "You proclaim peace, but practice violence, I want nothing more to do with you and your teachings!" Then, I left. This was a turning point in my 'belief,' even though I had yet to experience any truth or revelation from going to the mosque. I continued to attend, but now only infrequently.

My mother had some Catholic influence in her life, and my sisters went to Catholic schools. They would win prizes for their diligent work, and one such prize was a Bible. I use to read it on a regular basis and imitate the preachers on the radio as a form of entertainment. At that time of my youth, the radio was our only form of entertainment in our home—I remember my mother asking me if I wanted to be a preacher! Although I did not read the Word to know Christ, I believe the seed of the Word was being sown in my heart, and it was more life giving than reading or hearing words from the Koran.

I left home when I was nineteen years old to undertake nurse training in the UK. It was difficult to adjust to a completely new lifestyle, both from a religious and cultural experience, but it was here that my conversion began to grow roots. It started with a diet change, as I ate only a vegetarian diet for the first few weeks. This was in keeping with the Muslim's tradition of eating only halal products, but it was not possible to get halal products in the cafeteria. Thus, I started to eat chicken and beef, and felt no different for doing so!

As I began to make friends in a new country, I met two seminary students who were working in the hospital at that time. They introduced me to the Catholic Church. We began a dialogue about Christianity and other religions as I had read the entire Bible more than once in Guyana. Thus, we had some lively discussions, as we shared from personal experiences and beliefs. I was challenged by their sincerity, love and dedication to what they believed, but most importantly: their belief and desire to serve God was due to their faith in Him, and not out of obligation and fear as was so predominant in the Muslim faith.

I started to attend the Catholic Church on a regular basis, and was struck by the similarity in their devotion and rituals to a god that they could not see. However, there was a more 'life giving force' while attending this church, than I had experienced in the mosque, and it increased my desire to learn more about the God that they worshipped. At that time, the charismatic movement was spreading, and I became involved in one of their small groups. This movement had a deeper devotion to Christ, through the baptism of the Holy Spirit. My first impression was that they were delusional; just like some of my patients on the psychiatric units because they spoke in an unknown tongue, sang and praised their God. However, this did not deter me as I felt at peace in such an atmosphere. The people were also genuine in their love and devotion to God, and had a desire to serve Him. I was eventually baptized into the Catholic Church.

Later, I met my wife, and we became more involved in the charismatic movement. We moved to Cambridge, England, after getting married. It was here that my conversion to Christianity became more 'real,' with a deeper impact as I became 'born again,' through the ministry and teachings of another couple. This is an experience that is vital to any believer in Christ, in order to see the kingdom of God (John 3:3), and to have a deeper relationship with Jesus Christ. Up to this point in time, my conversion was based on knowledge with an inward peace, that I was serving a God who created and loved me. This born again experience gave me the realization that I was a sinner in need of a saviour, and Jesus Christ died on the cross to redeem me from such a state. This increased my desire to know more about God and to attend a Bible college.

We immigrated to Canada, and I eventually went to a Bible college in the US. My faith in Christ was deepened, and the Word became more alive with a deeper understanding of God. It also brought out this revelation: Christianity is not a religion, but a lifestyle and a relationship with Christ. You can only have a relationship with another person if that person is alive, and no other religion can proclaim such a fact.

ABOUT THE AUTHOR

Rad Khan was born in Georgetown, Guyana; but now lives in Toronto, Canada; and works as a registered nurse. He was a Muslim from birth, but accepted Christ as his Saviour. Rad graduated from C.F.N.I. in 1989, and completed a Bachelor of Theology degree in 1993. He has written two books: *L-S-D* and *The Mind-Field of Success or Defeat* – available at Amazon.com.

To learn more about Rad:
http://faithwriters.com/testimonies.php

DISILLUSIONMENT TO DELIGHT

By Dave Walker

I remember, as though it were yesterday, the night that would forever change my life. I had just moved to a mining town and, as the new doctor, was enjoying a welcoming party. As I celebrated with my latest friends, I felt a tap on my shoulder.

"Phone call for you, Dave."

Wondering who would call at that hour, I took the phone. "Hello."

On the other end, I heard my sister-in law, Erica. "I have some bad news. Ray's been in an accident."

Those words started a chain reaction that shattered my night. Shaking my head, I couldn't believe that my fun-loving brother was in an accident again. Last month he had borrowed my car and returned it with a dent. What now?

"Sorry to hear that, Erica. Is the car badly damaged? Is Ray hurt?"

"He is critical, Dave. They don't expect him to survive the night."

My world changed. My brother and I were very close. *Ray dying?* My head, already spinning from the alcohol, battled to make sense of it all.

A call to a colleague confirmed it; Ray could not survive. I flew to Cape Town the next day and identified his shattered body. Then, with my grieving parents and his pregnant wife, we buried my dear brother.

In the following weeks, I thought my heart would burst. Often, as

I sat in my consulting room, waves of sorrow suddenly erupted un-asked from deep inside. Uncontrollable tears overflowed and streamed down my face.

In the midst of that, there was a cold anger towards God and a deep disappointment in Him. How could He have allowed this? Wasn't He supposed to be a caring God? Brought up in a loving home, I considered myself a Christian even though I didn't pray or read my Bible. I always assumed God would look after me. Now, however, I doubted that. It seemed that He just watched from afar, and let us get on with our lives.

Two years later, Erica, my brother's wife, died from a sudden ill-ness making their little girl an orphan. Now I was convinced that God did not care. My wife and I adopted our niece.

Disappointed, but highly ambitious, I set about making a name for myself as an anesthesiologist, not worrying about whom I insult-ed or hurt on the way to the top.

I went to church occasionally, but merely because it was the re-spectable thing to do.

I had a special interest in Intensive Care and found it hugely sat-isfying being involved in hi-tech medicine while seeing my patients recover from life and death situations. Yet I wanted to give more, but was powerless to do so. In times of crisis, one needs invisible, spiritual support which I could not provide. I did not believe in a God who would help them.

It all came to a head when I received an urgent call.

"Come to the surgical theatre, Dave. We need to operate right away."

A man lay on the operating table, barely breathing, white from blood loss, shocked and sweating. I discovered later, that after a bout of drinking, he'd had a violent argument with his wife, stormed out of the house and he roared onto the freeway in his car. Appar-ently anger and alcohol caused him to lose control and crash.

We fought dramatically for his life in the operating room. Blood gushed from severed arteries, and his shattered organs needed to be repaired.

Finally things were brought under control, and I cared for him in the Intensive Care Unit.

"Well, if he gets out of this, I am sure he will have learned his lesson, and his lifestyle will improve," I thought.

Yet months later, after discharge, I heard that he was drinking more, and had divorced his wife.

The news hit me like a shock of cold water and made me question all I was doing. Suddenly it seemed futile. If I could care, but not change something in the hearts of my patients, then what was the point? I felt discouraged and disillusioned. I longed for a God who would be personal and powerful, but He still seemed distant and uncaring.

Shortly afterwards, at a particularly moving church service, I stayed behind to talk about my disappointment with God.

The couple I spoke to understood. "Maybe you are not allowing Him to intervene and guide your life," they said. "You seem self-sufficient and confident of your own ability. Why not ask for His help, even if you think you can do it yourself? Try praying and reading your Bible regularly."

In the following days, I did as they suggested. I read my Bible and tried to pray. At work I started asking God to help me and thanking Him when things went well. To be honest, it all seemed a bit unreal, but I did it anyway.

Four days later, God came!

I awoke early in the morning, bathed in the love of Jesus. His presence filled the room with a tangible sense of peace. I actually thought the Second Coming had arrived, and all were experiencing what I was. I knew without a doubt that He is personal, present with us, interested in what we do, and is waiting for us to include him, through prayers, in everything we do. I realised that, while He does not always shield us from the trials of life, He is always there to bring strength and comfort in those times if we will just continue to trust Him.

At work I started relating my experience, sharing the love of God with my patients and encouraging them to trust Him as they prepared for surgery.

I now prayed with my patients in the Intensive Care Unit. God showed just how personal and powerful He is when we call on Him. Some patients were healed; others encountered, in real life-changing ways, a loving God. I experienced what I had longed to see--not just bodies being healed, but lives changed on the inside as they felt the presence of God and learned to trust Him.

It has been an exciting walk, these last thirty-five years. It hasn't always been easy. I watched my darling wife of fourty years waste away from cancer, till finally she breathed her last breath. This time though, instead of rejecting God as I had done with my brother and his wife, I pressed in to Him. He made His presence known with a tangible strength and peace that was so real, but is difficult for me to describe.

The Bible is full of promises of blessing for those who trust in God to the end. I cannot say it is always easy when I go through trials I do not understand, but I know it is better than not trusting Him. I have experienced both.

Every time I am tempted to think God is distant or does not love me, I turn to Jesus and meditate on the Cross. When I think about what He went through for my sake, I cannot deny He loves me, despite anything I am going through that seems to point to the contrary. A love that gives like He did cannot be distant, so I choose to trust. He has never failed that trust to date, and I am sure He never will.

ABOUT THE AUTHOR

Dave Walker trained at the University of Cape Town Medical School and specialised in anaesthesia at Groote Schuur Hospital, Cape Town. He practiced in Pietermaritzburg, South Africa, for twenty-two years, where he was Administrative Head of Grey's Hospital ICU. Then he moved to the Middle East for six years during which time he was Head of the Anaesthetic Department at Tawam Hospital, United Arab Emirates.

Since retiring from anaesthesia, he writes and has published a book, *God in the ICU*, which tells of his experiences praying with his patients in the Intensive Care Unit.

He currently lives in Cape Town. He is married to Margie and has three daughters and seven grandchildren of his own and stepsons, stepdaughters and a step-granddaughter from Margie.

He is a keen member of Faithwriters.

To learn more about Dave Walker see:
http://faithwriters.com/testimonies.php

FINDING PEACE

By Matthew Guddat

I can't remember much about the night that would forever alter my life. Street lamps shimmered through the truck window as we turned a corner. I sat high up in the front cabin, squeezed between my mother and a rather large man who was our chauffer. We were due north of a home neither my mother nor I had ever been to before.

I can't remember crossing the English border into Scotland, boarding the ferry, or being carried in my mother's arms to our new home because I was merely a few years old at the time. Why my mother chose to leave my father is a vague area for me, and one I have felt little desire to pry into. Needless to say, she was devastated in the process.

My mother found work as a cleaner and later as an office worker. In hindsight, I can see how my mother struggled, yet she was a God-fearing woman who labored, if not for herself, then for her young son. She encouraged me with her words. "Never give up, Matthew."

The Western Islands of Scotland are everything you could imagine them to be. The summers are beautiful, though short, and the winters are long and dark, threatening the Scots with wild and abandoned weather patterns. It was a normal occurrence for the winds to blow so strong that houses would lose their roofs; boats in the harbor would come loose from their moorings and crash against the rocks; trees would fall; and rivers burst their banks. Scary? Maybe for some, but not for a young boy; I loved it. It whispered adventure.

Despite an ideal childhood setting, I could never handle the torment of my parents' broken relationship. Sometimes at night, with tears in my eyes, I would plead with my mother to reconcile with my dad. Rational replies never seemed to provide much comfort. I wanted *both* of my parents, and I often felt powerless, confused, and unable to do anything about it. It wasn't long before resentment wiled its way into my heart. I resented my mother for leaving and my father for his absence. Why couldn't they work it out?

My teenage years were a testing time. After many years of watering seeds of resentment and bitterness, I no longer related such feelings to my parents' divorce. Anger was fast becoming a way of life, though I was blind to it. It rested upon my shoulders like a heavy jacket. With resentment and hatred well rooted, I lost care and respect for my mother. It wasn't long before the appeal of escape wooed me.

I loved drugs at first; they were fun and kept my anger at bay. I still remember cold winter nights spent with my friends laughing, drinking, and escaping. A cold chill runs down my back when I relive those years in my mind.

My mother spilled tears over my rebellion. I remember coming home often to find her weeping in deep grief as I spat harsh words at her. There was no longer the smell of freshly cooked meals in our home or the sound of happy chatter. The television acted as a painkiller for my mother and me. In its dim light, we could avoid conversation and pretend our life didn't oppress us.

The drugs I took never maintained their promises. With them, came a lifestyle of addiction, stealing, law breaking, fighting, and the occasional police officer at the door. Soon that all too familiar heaviness was back to stay and more threatening than before. Over time I bent toward depression and self-harm. Anger and bitterness ruled my thoughts, and my feelings spilled onto those around me. I was in the grip of a prison that I could not escape, nor did I know how to, or if it were even possible. Many nights I would lie in bed and muffle my cries with a pillow *desperate* to break free.

After one particular schoolyard fight, I was admitted to the hospital where my mother worked. She no longer could bear the pain of seeing her only son ruining his life. In haste, and out of desperation, I was sent away from home to live with family friends. Had I gone too far this time?

The family took me in as their own son, yet my habits and heaviness remained. One evening, they insisted I join them for a church service. I resisted, but was left no choice when they squeezed me into their sedan and locked the house.

I scorned all the happy people surrounding me. They knew nothing of what I was carrying, and I was not about to share it with them. I sunk into my chair and listened reluctantly. It was at this point something happened. To this day I cannot recall the preacher's sermon; however, I can assure you that as I listened, something clicked.

Jesus is real. He *is* real.

I returned home to see an all too familiar sight; my mother sat with her head in her hands weeping uncontrollably. She looked up at my face with distant eyes and spoke words that cut deep into my soul, "I thought you would be a blessing to me Matthew, but you're a curse."

Nothing can describe the nausea that swept over me. *I was a curse? Truly?* I could not fight or cry that nausea away. My mother had given so much for me and had finally given up. Even she could not love me anymore. As I lay in my bed, the torment returned. Depression lingered overhead. I don't know how long it was; it seemed like an eternity, but after a while I became aware of another presence in my room. Though I could not see Him, I knew beyond a doubt that Jesus was standing in my bedroom. In my desperation I cried out, *"God... please help me!"*

Fear pulsated through my body like lightning. I was no longer blind. I could see everything now. I could see how I had nurtured my bitterness; welcomed hatred and resentment; and how I had hurt so many people– including my mother–*my mother!* I was terrified. Surely God would punish me. Then, unexpectedly…

Peace.

I wish I could put into words the contrast between years of heaviness, confusion, anger, depression, and then ... the presence of peace. It is like a violent ocean being calmed or a downpour in the desert–undeserving, yet more real to me now than the touch of my own skin.

My mother and I soon reconciled, and our tears were turned to joy as we began a new relationship with each other, one of honor and love. I also visited my Dad in England, and we now have a great relationship. We enjoy getting to know one another. Many years have passed since I cried out to Jesus. The freedom that came all those years ago is just as alive today as it was then.

ABOUT THE AUTHOR

Matthew Guddat was born in England, raised in Scotland, and immigrated to New Zealand after his schooling years. He spent five years as a missionary around Asia and the Pacific region, and now serves as a youth pastor and works in a local bookshop. His wife, Leigh, is a registered nurse. They have been married for three happy years, and live together in Whangarei, Northland, New Zealand.

Read more from Matthew:
http://faithwriters.com/testimonies.php

From Dare to Eternity

By Dannie Hawley

Wearing my favorite church dress, bright orange covered by a layer of fine lace, I paced the short hallway and glanced frequently through the curtained glass of my front door. My circular doilie-like head covering rested securely in my pocket, bobby pin at the ready.

But what did people wear when the meeting was in someone's home and not the church? When I'd accepted Rey's dare to celebrate his birthday with his Bible Study, I forgot to ask him about the head-covering.

Imagine him thinking I was afraid to go to his Bible Study. Hmpf! Well, after tonight, he'd see I wasn't afraid; I just had no interest in being anything other than a Catholic.

He met me at the door. "Wow, you're lookin' good there," he said. "Ready to go?"

So far, so good. At least, when he saw my outfit he didn't frown.

"I'm ready. Remember, I'm only going because it's your birthday. You'll stop asking me to go to this Bible Study after tonight, right?"

"Yeah, I know that's the deal. Let's go." He grinned so wide.

When we arrived at the meeting, I fingered the little lace head-covering in my pocket, took a deep breath and stepped over the kitchen-door threshold. The delicious aroma of just-baked chocolate cake wafted through the room. But a quick glance at the attire of the host couple overrode the mouth-watering scent of the promised dessert. I clenched the lace in my pocket, my jaw tightened, I wanted to

26

bolt.

The closer I got to the living room with its raucous chatter, the bigger the cannonball in my stomach grew. *God, help me not throw up.* All around the periphery of the room, in chairs or on the carpeted floor, kids my age were dressed in jeans or shorts and tee shirts.

My roommate and Rey's girlfriend, Joyce, indicated an empty seat next to her, and I sank into it. I looked around, but didn't see a priest or someone who looked like a minister, so I assumed he was late.

"Okay, let's get started," Bob said, circling the room with his eyes and wide grin. "We have a guest today for Rey's birthday. Her name is Dannie, and we want to make her feel welcome. She's never been to a Bible Study so we told her she could just watch and listen this time."

Welcomes and *glad-you're-heres* echoed around the room.

I smiled and nodded.

"Okay, anyone have any praise reports to share?" Bob said.

Shuffling feet, friendly elbow jabs, and mumbles encouraged a few young members to stand up, step up, and speak up. I figured this was the way they bought more time for the minister, who had yet to appear.

Soon I was caught up in the group's excitement. Each of the young adults spoke of a need that had been brought before the group on some past occasion, and then each one told a marvelous account of God's divine response to the prayers.

I just couldn't imagine it. The Almighty God of the universe was hearing the prayers of these college kids and answering them?

"Okay, some really marvelous testimonies there; isn't our God great!" Bob took up his Bible.

Lots of hoots and howls erupted from the group. It sounded more like a sports event than a church.

Bob read some Scriptures and talked about them a little. Then he encouraged us to meditate on them throughout the week. Next his fiancée stood, grabbed a stack of little slips of white paper, and

27

passed them around the room.

"Write your prayer requests for this week on the slips," she said. "You can put your name on or not. Fold it, and put it in the bowl when it comes around."

Joyce offered me a paper, and I shook my head and let the little pile of paper slips pass me. How I wanted to write something on the paper. I did need prayer, but I didn't know what to write.

Help me! I don't know what you're doing here, but I want to see God answer my prayers like that, too!

Instead, I just sat, arms tightly folded across my chest, watching.

When the bowl made a second pass, each participant took a slip of folded paper from the bowl. All week the students would pray for the requests represented on the papers they drew. I didn't, of course, since I hadn't contributed.

When Bob said next week we'd see what God would do, everyone clapped and cheered.

After the whole group prayed for a couple of kids with special requests, it was time to pray for the birthday guy, and bring on the cake and ice cream. An older guy never did show up.

When that *Amen!* resounded around that circle of hungry early twenty-somethings, I had only one thing on my mind, and it wasn't chocolate cake. Something had happened to me in that meeting, and I didn't understand it at all. I felt like I'd entered the whirling winds of a hurricane, being twisted and bounced around in all directions at once.

I begged Rey to take me home.

Rey begged me to stay.

I begged more, and he finally gave up and took me home.

My trembling hands turned the key in my apartment door, and barreling through the doorway, I ran into the room that was both bedroom and living room. My crucifix hung on the wall next to the fireplace. Just the sight of it started the flood of tears.

I knelt under the crucifix and cried into my hands. "God, oh God. Did I do something wrong in going there?" More tears. "I only wanted to make Rey stop asking me, and it was his birthday, and if I was wrong to go, I'm sorry. But, God, those kids... those kids seemed to know You. I want to know You, too!"

The torrent of tears increased until anything I wanted to say to God would have to be a communication of thoughts; I couldn't speak at all. Funny enough, it felt like the flow of tears was coming from the deepest reaches of my insides, not my eyes. It was as if my eyes were only a passageway, but the origin was much deeper.

As I wept, I became aware of God's thoughts streaming through my mind. Things about forgiveness and acceptance. I sensed that all of the sins of my past were being forgiven right there and then.

I thanked the Lord in my thoughts, still weeping too hard for speech. I asked God to come into my life as He had done for those kids who had shared. I gave my life to God and asked Him to help me do whatever it was He wanted me to do.

When I stood again, I had the most unbelievable peace flowing out of my innermost being. I never ever felt so good, so clean and totally new. I didn't know what had happened to me there on my knees, but I do know that it changed my entire life forever.

The following Tuesday, clad in tee shirt and jeans, I returned to claim what was to become my regular spot on the floor.

ABOUT THE AUTHOR

Dannie Hawley, a native of Eastern Montana, is a pediatric nurse practitioner, who has served in foreign missionary service since 1984, primarily in Africa. Since 2007, Dannie has worked as the project director of the Samaritan House Children's Center, located in the Republic of Guinea, West Africa.

You can learn more about this author at:
http://faithwriters.com/testimonies.php

FROM SLAVERY TO FREEDOM

By Kathleen Trissel

Insecurity

"How do I know if Christ has come into my life?" That was the question I asked the Christian counselor at the alcohol-and-drug-treatment center in 1982. When I completed the program, I went home and read the gospel tracts she gave me, and I prayed to receive Christ. I didn't feel any different, didn't know if he wanted me, and didn't understand that I needed to receive Christ by faith.

She then asked, "Did you ask him?"

I declared, "Yes."

Confessing Christ openly made it real and brought it alive in my heart, but insecurity marked many years of my walk with Christ. To complicate matters, when I saw the preacher focus more on himself than on Christ, I left the church. The experience left me disillusioned with the formal church.

Still longing for emotional connectedness with people, I turned back to the gay community, and even attended a gay church. With persistence, I sought to reconcile a faithful and committed relationship with another woman while still convincing myself that I was following the Word of God. False peace quieted the turmoil for a while.

Lies I Believed

Lies about myself, lies about homosexuality, and lies about God's Word plagued me. I even received a "revelation." It went like this: Suppose God intended everyone to speak Hebrew, but because of the Tower of Babel (see Genesis chapter 11), God confused the language of the people so they could not glorify themselves by building a tower to Heaven. I agreed that in God's perfect plan, he did not want me to have homosexual desires, but because we live in a fallen world, that's how I was born. Therefore, why would God reject my homosexual lifestyle, if I were born that way, any more than he would reject someone who spoke a language other than Hebrew?

I learned later that God's truth about homosexuality was always in his Word, but I wasn't seeking truth. I was looking for the answer I wanted to hear. The devil was happy to provide me with a "revelation."

Though I was a wandering soul, I longed for intimacy with Christ. I even wrote letters to God while sitting at the bar. Out of the pain and brokenness of my heart and life, I began to seek and cry out for intimacy with Christ. One night in 1992, when I came out of the bar at closing, the Holy Spirit met me with the conviction to return to Christ. The Bible I had felt was too holy to touch, I now returned to reading and taking into my heart.

False Identity

The reasons for a person's vulnerability to homosexuality are many. Jeffrey Satinover addresses some of these in his book, *Homosexuality and the Politics of Truth*. Contributing factors include: genetics, personality, abuse as a child, and childhood relationships with adults, to name just a few. A pastor I talked with suggested that abuse as a child contributed to the homosexuality, but I told him the reason didn't matter. It was my identity. I didn't believe I could be free.

Next, I went through a time where I had no peace of mind. Opening the Bible, I tried to reconcile homosexuality with God, but I couldn't do it this time. I always had taken passages out of context, which had quieted the gnawing in my spirit. This time felt different. I read 1 Corinthians 6:9-11, which says: *"Do you not know that the wicked will not inherit the kingdom of God? Do not be deceived: Neither the sexually immoral nor idolaters nor adulterers nor male prostitutes nor homosexual offenders nor thieves nor the greedy nor drunkards nor slanderers nor swindlers will inherit the kingdom of*

God. And that is what some of you were. But you were washed, you were sanctified, you were justified in the name of the Lord Jesus Christ and by the Spirit of our God."

The words jumped off the page, especially the word *were* in verse 11. Others, caught in a homosexual lifestyle, had gone before me and now enjoyed freedom. I became hopeful. I now believed, that by God's grace, he could restore natural desires in my life and open the prison door that enslaved me.

I struggled with letting go of my identity as a homosexual and the pride I felt because I was different. I asked for God's forgiveness and healing, and told him I didn't understand why he was so merciful to me. I heard these words in my mind without knowing it was part of the Scripture verse found in Romans 9:15: *"I will have mercy on whom I will have mercy..."*

The derailed journey that began in 1982, though painful, has met with a deeper intimacy with Christ than I ever imagined possible. Philippians 1:6 encouraged me by letting me know that God takes responsibility to complete the work he initiates. *"And I am sure of this, that he who began a good work in you will bring it to completion at the day of Jesus Christ."*(ESV)

The Process

Freedom and transformation into the image of Christ is a process, which happens as I set my affection on Christ and on things above, not on the problem. Colossians 3:1-2 became my theme verses: *"Since, then, you have been raised with Christ, set your hearts on things above, where Christ is seated at the right hand of God. Set your minds on things above, not on earthly things."* As long as I focused on the problem, it intensified, but as I focused on Jesus, my feelings slowly changed. Jesus carried me through gut-wrenching emotional pain as he brought healing to my heart and life.

The Lord also exposed the lies I received about myself and the homosexual lifestyle. Exposing lies, however, was not enough; it also took a willingness to receive God's truth. In brokenness, the Lord brought healing.

True Identity

As I read and studied the Bible, God planted holy longings in my heart. Now I long for the day when I will behold him in all his glory, see him face-to-face, and fall on my face in everlasting worship of my King. I know that I'm a child of the King, born-again into the royal bloodline of Christ, his princess; that's my identity. My identity is in Christ who rescued me for his glory.

Although I long to be with him in my Heavenly home, until then he's given me a heart to worship him, to encourage believers, and to show lost souls the way to life in him. *"For to me to live is Christ, and to die is gain."* (Philippians 1:20)

What's the message then? There is hope, forgiveness, healing, and freedom in Christ alone. Do you long for that hope and freedom? Seeking hard after Christ brings the reward of intimacy with him, which is worth all it costs. If this is your desire, begin asking, seeking, knocking, and praying to Jesus. He will hear and answer because he rewards all those who seek him diligently.

*All Bible quotes are from the New International Version, except where noted.

ABOUT THE AUTHOR

Kathleen A. Trissel is a freelance writer from Canton, Ohio, USA. She has publication credits in numerous non-fiction Christian publications. She also served as Editor for the *Daughters Journal*, a publication that goes into women's prisons.

She holds a B.A. in English and Psychology and an M.A. in Counseling and Human Development. Her passion is to reach those who do not know Christ with the glorious gospel, and to encourage believers to grow in a love relationship with Jesus.

To read more of her work, go to:
http://faithwriters.com/testimonies.php

From Suicide to Singing

By Rick L. King

From suicide to singing
Yes, this is my story:
Of how Jesus came to me
In all of His glory.

I met Jesus
At age twenty-eight
When all hope was gone
And death was my fate.

I was married
To a beautiful wife.
I had a house.
And a desire for life.

I had a good job
And money to spend.
Yet, I didn't have peace
Way down deep within.

I tried through sex
All of my needs to fulfill.
I tried through drugs,
But my life was empty still.

I tried to buy
Fulfillment within,
But all that I accomplished
Was to go deep into sin.

The next thing I knew,
My wife and I were apart.
My job was gone,
And I had a broken heart.

All the dreams that I'd had
And all of my many plans
Seemed to just all blow away
Like the drifting of the sands.

My nerves were shot.
I started to shake.
I was throwing up blood,
So nerve pills, I did take.

I couldn't eat or sleep
Because of the pain inside.
So then to the booze
I tried to escape in, and hide.

No matter what I tried
Nothing turned out well.
Back then I didn't know
That I was bound for Hell.

There was nothing left
For me to do.
So I decided to end it all
For there was just no use.

I had it all planned out
Just how my suicide would be
But I came to find out
That someone had a plan for me.

I found myself going
To a couple of friends.
They had always loved me
And had never condemned.

They told me of Jesus
And of His love for me
And how He died upon the Cross
At Calvary.

They said that if I would ask Jesus
To forgive all my sin
And ask Him into my heart
That I would be Born Again.

Then, all the sudden,
New peace filled my heart
For Jesus had saved me.
He gave me a new start.

I went out of their door
And looked all around.
It was hard to comprehend
All that I had found.

The trees and the sky
Were a new beautiful sight
For the darkness was gone
I was seeing through the light.

Yes, this was far beyond
All of my thinking
For Jesus had taken me
From Suicide to Singing.

ABOUT THE AUTHOR

Rick is from Oregon, USA. He met Jesus over thirty years ago. He was considering suicide when Jesus found him and gave him a reason to live. Because he didn't have the answer then, it has made it easier to know that the only way to truly live is in Jesus. *"Then he answered and spake unto me, saying, This is the word of the LORD unto Zerubbabel, saying, Not by might, nor by power, but by my spirit, saith the LORD of hosts."* *(Zechariah 4:6 KJV)*

Learn more about this author and read one of his many books for free: http://faithwriters.com/testimonies.php

Going the Distance

By Ennis Smith

Hearing the family van park in the driveway, I typed out the last words of my text message. I pressed SEND, and stuffed the phone into my pocket. My wife, Misty, opened the front door, glanced in my direction, then diverted her eyes elsewhere.

"Hey," she said, disinterested.

"'Sup," I replied casually.

"So…can we talk? I have something on my mind."

"Sure, what's—" My phone buzzed. A return text had come in.

"No, not right now. Besides, someone needs you, obviously." She pointed toward my buzzing pocket. "Maybe we can go out tomorrow for a drink."

As she walked away, I reached for the phone.

She's a liar, and you need to leave her, read the message from a female colleague. Recently, I had taken to confiding in her regarding my marriage. *You can do so much better, Ennis. You deserve someone who can take care of you.*

The next day, Misty and I drove to the riverfront. We walked along the boardwalk making small talk for a while.

"All right, we're here, Smith." I turned toward her. "What's on your mind?"

"Our marriage," she said solemnly. "I think…maybe…we should try separating for a while."

And there it was. We were now talking about the pink elephant in the living room.

"It's really not… you. I just think I need time to myself to discover who I am, and where I need to be." She stared out over the

38

gray rippling waters of late fall.

I didn't put up a fight. I agreed to the separation. In truth, I was tired of the nagging feeling that my wife might have embraced a life of infidelity. I had also begun to believe in the soothing words of my newfound confidant, who continuously shared her own marital problems with me. Our stories were similar, and I had come to view her as a shoulder to lean on.

Two days later, my fears were proven correct. The phone bill arrived. I scrutinized Misty's cellphone portion and discovered dozens of calls made to a specific number over the past month. I dialed that number, and my heart sank when a familiar voice from her past answered the call. It was *him*. The man I'd had to deal with almost ten years past. Once again, it seemed he'd returned to her life. I couldn't speak; I could only end the call with a trembling hand. Hurt immediately turned to rage. I called her, demanding an explanation, and insisting on a divorce.

"I want you out of my house!" I yelled. "If you want to be with this idiot so badly, you can leave tonight. I'll let the kids know you won't be coming home."

"You can't take my kids a—" she started.

I abruptly ended the call. Spitefully, I gathered up our five children and announced our divorce. The three oldest were rocked to the core, understanding fully what that meant for the family. The youngest two didn't understand. Having to explain divorce to my three- and six-year-old children only intensified my rage toward Misty.

She never left the house, and for a week, we tip-toed around one another. I spent most of my time drinking myself into a stupor to cope while she openly continued her separate life. One weekend, we sat in our bedroom and talked candidly about our failing marriage.

"I can't understand why you just can't be honest with me," I said.

"You want the truth? I don't know why I don't love you anymore," she said. "I don't even know why I see other men. That's right, other men. It's not just one. I think I love him, but I'm also

39

seeing his best friend, unbeknown to him. I can't stop it."

My knees buckled, and I collapsed to the floor. My pride broke, and I cried out to God. In that instant, I rationalized that this whole situation was payback for the thousands of indiscretions I had perpetuated over the years. I had once given my heart to the Lord, but had backslidden and become worse than before. I'd lied to my wife, behaved selfishly, cheated and stolen to get my way, so many times. I deserved everything that was transpiring now. My tears flowed, and I pleaded with God for forgiveness. I apologized to Him for everything I had done.

Two weeks later, I found a small home to rent. My wife had settled for an upper flat to move into. As we packed our belongings and prepared to go our separate ways, she came to me one afternoon.

"Dear, are we doing the right thing?" Her eyes seemed so sincere, but emotionally, I had already departed from her.

"Yeah, I think we are. People divorce every day. The kids will adapt."

"Can we try one last time? I think maybe we should give church a try."

I was appalled at the idea. It was the fact that *she* had come up with it. I stalled for time, having already fixed my mind on starting a new life without her.

"Sure. I guess a few visits wouldn't hurt."

****

Six months later, Jesus recaptured my heart. Up to that day, we had church-hopped until settling on a large congregational Pentecostal church. I struggled to accept the worship music, and often fought against the messages of the pastor. Because of my hardheartedness, our marriage sputtered along slowly. By all appearances, we were fine: still in the same house together, still one big family. But, we each fought our personal demons, maintaining one foot in the world while trying out Christianity. And then it happened.

I attended a men's ministry meeting, one Wednesday evening. The speaking guest, Bill, was the author of a small book entitled, *30 Minutes in Hell*. During the altar call, I reluctantly approached, fell to my knees and immediately felt the sensation of burning pressure fighting to remain over me. I remember pounding my fists on the altar. Bill approached and laid a hand on my shoulder.

"Woo!" he screamed. "Brother, I don't know what you've got going on, but some burden you've carried for a long time is lifting off you, right now. Don't fight it! Let that thing go!"

It was hard, but I did. I released years' worth of misguided anger against my wife, that very night. God set me free, and almost immediately I saw a change in our marriage.

On January 31, 2010, Misty and I were baptized together. For a few months afterward, Satan came against us with vengeance. Misty struggled to sever ties with other men, and I struggled with forgiveness, drinking, and releasing my own negative ties. But we maintained our dedication to the Lord, and He has continued to strengthen our marriage and family.

Recently, I got the chance to witness our two youngest children, now seven and ten years old, raise their hands unabashedly in worship to the Lord. I cried tears of joy, knowing the Lord blesses and keeps us.

On our return home from the two-day children's rally, my wife wrapped her arms around me and hugged me close. "I didn't realize how much I loved you until you were gone away from me."

"Me too. I really missed you."

Today, I'm giving God the praise for helping us to go the distance.

ABOUT THE AUTHOR

Ennis C. Smith lives in Lincoln Park, Michigan (U.S.A.) with his wife, Misty, and their five children. By day, he works as an engineering technician for a Metro Detroit engineering firm. As an aspiring author, Ennis hopes to spread the gospel through story and testimony.

Read more from Ennis:
http://faithwriters.com/testimonies.php

HEARING GOD'S GENTLE VOICE

By Donna Mae Carrico

I have not had an easy life. My earliest memories were full of incest, sexual, emotional, and physical abuse. I am sure there are many people dealing with similar things in life. As a child, I was sent to a church and learned about a loving God from a wonderful Sunday school teacher. My understanding of salvation was that I had to be good; however, this belief is wrong. As I became a teen-ager, I felt dirty, guilty, and wretched. Thinking I was pregnant by my biological father, I took an overdose of pills and tried to commit suicide. I just slept them off while my parents ignored the fact that something was wrong with me. I remember thinking that there must be some reason God kept me from dying, so I just had to get on with life. To make matters worse, I confided in my boyfriend about the abuse, and then he raped me. Then, the one time I reached out for help and tried to tell my pastor what was really going on at home, he made sexual advances as well.

I was trained to be a victim. The enemy of God has a way of get-ting into our minds and inflicting a false guilt on children who are sexually abused. I tried to say, "No," but was not strong enough to fight off the abuse. I felt guilty because I couldn't stop the abuse. I thought that no one would have believed me if I told because my parents were upstanding citizens of the community. There was no way to escape because I wasn't old enough to drive. My parents forbade me to hang out with friends. Like many abusers, they isolat-ed me so I couldn't tell anyone the family secret.

I married to get away from home before I began to deal with my past. I was blessed with two beautiful children. My first marriage, of almost thirteen years, ended with the last year and a half speckled with promiscuity, alcohol, and getting involved with a satanic cult. It ended in divorce and another suicide attempt. When I would go out drinking and come home, I had the Bible laying by my bed. I would search it for answers. God kept pulling at me, but I went right back out and did it again. Once again, however, God kept me alive. On my second suicide attempt, I cut my wrists with a razor blade over and over, but God miraculously closed the skin so I could not bleed to death. I even tried to walk in front of a train, and it mysteriously slowed down. I began to realize again that it was not my time to die. I hid that insight in my heart. I knew I was a miserable, adulteress at the end of my rope with nowhere to turn; yet God loved me enough to keep me from dying. I praise God that he watched over me and came to me when I was in the depths of despair with my life in such turmoil.

Finally one day, an old high school friend of mine, Marsha, came to my business and said, "You know, Donna, Jesus is standing there with His arms opened just waiting for you."

I hung my head. "I'm too bad of a person. I've done so many despicable things. Jesus will never accept me."

She still insisted I go to her church. When I went, the Lord spoke to me as I really heard the true salvation message of God's forgiveness, grace, and mercy. God spoke to me in His gentle voice and said, "Let me help you carry your burdens; you've been carrying them long enough."

I heard Him and, with many tears of sorrow, was born again on December 2, 1979. I felt His overwhelming peace come into my new life. In Romans 5:8-10, it reveals that God loved us, even when we were sinners. Then, in John 3:8-10, it explains that we must be born again. We learn we cannot work our way into Heaven in Titus 3:5 and in Ephesians 2:8-10.

Two weeks after being saved, I poured out my heart to God and told him I needed a companion. The next day, there was a knock at the door. My Sunday school teacher, David, stood there. "Hello, Donna, you know I've been thinking we are in the same boat. I have prayed for someone to go out to eat with, or to a movie, and to study the Bible with."

Those were the very same words I had prayed during the night. Could God answer my prayers that fast? I had barely spoken to my Sunday school teacher. I didn't even know he knew I existed. In my heart, I pondered the wonders of God, and just maybe, thought it might be the answer to my prayer. It was still hard to believe.

David began to share with me how he had been praying the night before. He told me, "I've always wanted a family, but it never has worked out. I was praying over Psalm 68 where it talks of setting the solitary in families. God doesn't want people to be lonely, so he provides them with families. God spoke to me and said, 'Donna is your family. Go to her and tell her.'"

I am sixty-five now, and that was thirty-three years ago on March 20, 2013. We are truly blessed. We have undeniable proof that God wanted us together. *Thank you, Lord, for giving me my beloved.* We started our ministry, Followers of Jesus Christ, Inc., shortly after our marriage to expose the darkness in cults and false religions, and to offer healing to survivors of many types of abuse. We continue to minister in many different areas, and now offer resources and have a 24/7 Internet Radio on our website.

My journey of healing and restoration has not always been easy. There have been plenty of physical challenges, but serving Jesus and having Him as my friend and Savior has given me hope and an exciting life. I process my memories by writing poems and offering them up to God for closure. I praise God for saving me and for being with me through all of my continuing trials in life. I look forward to spending eternity with Him.

Although it was written by King David many years before my conversion, Psalms 40:1-17 mirrors my pleas for God to hear me. King David is often called "a man after God's heart." He simply admitted his faults, told God about those who persecuted him, and asked for forgiveness, mercy, and justification. That is still my cry today in my walk with Him. *Thank you, Lord, for sparing my life.* I challenge you, reader, to accept the grace and mercy of God and be "born again."

ABOUT THE AUTHOR

Donna Mae Carrico ministers through guest speaking for conferences, radio, TV, her Internet radio program and books. Along with her husband, David, she authored nineteen books, and they minister to the world from their website and home in the United States. She has authored several articles, a book about prophecy, and is currently compiling her next book of short stories.

Read more from Donna:
http://faithwriters.com/testimonies.php

INFECTION OF EVIL

By Lynn Gipson

Having grown up with evil all around me, I know it can be infectious. As a child, I experienced evil when a trusted adult abused me physically and emotionally. It filled me with shame, fear, anger, and a sense of hopelessness. That infection invaded my life, making it almost impossible for me to love or trust others. Over time, I began to loathe myself. Something inside of me whispered, "You are unlovable, unworthy and a burden to others." That something was named Evil.

My antibiotic for this infection was found in Jesus Christ. He was the cure for my seemingly incurable infection. When I was washed in His blood, the infection died, and I was reborn with the pure soul God gave me when I came into this world. He not only gave me my soul back, but also my life.

When we give our symptoms of evil to Christ, He turns the fear into faith, the shame into glory, the anger into forgiveness, and the loathing into love. It is as simple as that. My life is a living testimony to all I have written here. I can honestly tell you I lived in fear every day for fifty-eight years of my life until the day I almost died from a brain tumor. A few days later, I was told I had stage four colon cancer. That was my "come to Jesus' time." At the time, I thought it was the end of the road, but it was only the beginning.

I dropped to my knees and asked Jesus to love me, and I immediately felt His loving presence. A warmth and sense of peace came over me, and I cried to Him and poured out my heart, asking forgiveness for my symptoms of evil.

After that, I was able to let go of the fear, shame, anger, and loathing and give it all to Jesus. I had no other choice, you see, because I thought I was dying, and I wanted to go to a better place than the one I was in.

Jesus took me to a better place, but I did not die. Four and a half years later, I am alive and, at the moment, cancer-free. I am also happier than I have ever been. My life is not perfect and certainly not without its challenges, but now I live with a faith so strong that nothing, and I mean nothing, is too big for me and my Savior to overcome.

From the onset of seizures that announced my brain tumor, right through the surgery that followed, and still throughout subsequent surgeries for colon, and then, uterine cancer, Jesus carried me. He held me through six weeks of hospitalizations, and gripped me tighter when I developed an infection from being in the hospital so long. He picked me up off the floor when a year of chemotherapy knocked me off my feet, and then miracle of all miracles, He healed me.

In four years, the cancer that was supposed to take my life has only made four minor reappearances. They were quickly taken care of with laser surgery. I don't know what the future holds for me as far the cancer goes, but I have almost learned to look forward to the challenge because my life is in the hands of the greatest Physician who ever lived. I fear neither life nor death.

It just occurred to me that I must have lived all of my life in order to write these words, hoping someone will read them and realize there is hope for the hopeless, and that miracles do happen. There is a way out and a road to real happiness. The way home is just a sincere prayer away, and the journey starts when one takes a step towards Jesus Christ.

My time here on earth is uncertain, but my body is cancer-free and my soul is free of the infection of Evil. Jesus Christ did that for me, not because I deserve it, but because He loves me.

ABOUT THE AUTHOR

Lynn Gipson is a sixty-two year old cancer survivor. She began writing a year ago and has finally found her purpose in life after all these years. She is now a published author of two short stories and several poems. She is a Christian and writes stories, poems, and articles of a Christian or spiritual nature. She lives in Mississippi and has one wonderful son and two amazing granddaughters, ages six and ten.

To read more of Lynn's work, go to:
http://faithwriters.com/testimonies.php

OUT OF THE SHADOWS

By Dorci Harris

My little sister and I followed the other two kids down the long wooden staircase, taking the steps one at time. I searched the room as we made our way down. A bare light bulb revealed a hollow, unfinished basement. While the other two showed us their toys, I could only think about what was going on upstairs.

We had passed the kitchen table on our way down, and I caught a glimpse of a Ouija board. *What were our mothers doing up there?* Maybe it was that we had been relegated to a basement filled with shadows lurking in countless corners with the door closed behind us. Maybe it was instinctual. But even with as few years as I had, it gave me goose bumps.

In the years after, my mother became obsessed with the supernatural. Our house was filled with tarot cards, Edgar Cayce books, dream interpretations, and the belief that spirits roamed our house. My childhood was swallowed up inside this deep, dark pit. What lined the walls were my parents' mental illnesses.

At home, I was lost in the blurry worlds of my mother's drug abuse and my father's alcoholism. I was being bullied at school, and felt pressure to maintain a façade of normalcy. No one knew that on the inside, I was crumbling.

Fear kept finding its way into the cracks and crevices of our home like a black mold growing out of control. When I was eleven, that fear came in the form of a male relative who preyed on little girls.

From time to time, I'd think back to that day in the basement and wonder where the game ended and reality began. I'd wake up in the dark of the night, paralyzed by fear. The fear lodged in the deepest recesses of my soul like wet cement that began to harden into anger. Cement is good for building walls, and there would be many bricks to come. In the middle of all that darkness, however, there was a quiet, powerful Light.

My parents moved us to a little orange house in a small, quiet neighborhood tucked away in the desert mountains. Moving there wasn't a coincidence. It was divine appointment.

I had a friend who lived at the end of our street and I often played at her house. Those were blessed times of peace. Sometimes, I'd be asked to sleep over. Her mother would tuck us in bed, and I saw what it was like for a mother to love her daughter.

When those sleepovers happened to be on Saturday nights, I'd be invited to go to church. My friend's dad was a pastor. I don't remember what was said during those services, but I know there was truth swirling around my spirit, finding its way in. I've often wondered if her parents prayed for me. I think they did.

Then there was the little church down the street. My mother took my sister and me and dropped us off there on Sunday mornings and Wednesday nights. I don't know if she was just trying to get rid of us for a while or if she was genuinely interested in our spiritual well-being. Whichever her motive, God had a plan.

The truth I heard at my friend's church had pierced something inside. It softened that cement just enough to let more truth find its way into my heart.

I helped in the nursery which was a child's stone's throw from the sanctuary. One Sunday morning, I crept closer to hear what was going on inside.

It was near the end of the message, and the pastor was saying that Jesus loved us. That was an incredible thought. *Could God really love me?* The pastor said that Jesus came to die for our sins and that the only way to Heaven was by believing in Him as the Son of God. If we put our faith in Him as Lord, then we would be saved. Somehow, I knew it was true. There would be a baptism soon.

I went home so excited that I could hardly keep quiet, but I had to wait for the safest possible time to ask my mother's permission to be baptized. I walked to the threshold of the little room one day when things were relatively calm, and she was preoccupied doing the laundry.

"Mom, um, can I get baptized?"

She didn't bother looking up, and that was fine with me. "Why?"

I took a deep breath. "Because I believe Jesus is the Son of God, and He died for my sins."

She thought for a long minute or two, and gave a sigh. "Okay."

It was Sunday morning–the big day! We all climbed in the car. Even my dad was coming. I lined up behind the others and was baptized. Things would be better, I thought. I just knew it...but nothing changed in the years that followed. In fact, the pit would get much deeper and darker before I would see the light.

About a month after my high school graduation, my mother, in a fit of rage, threw me out of the house late at night. I called my boyfriend, and he picked me up at the little church down the street.

I didn't see my parents for months. Years later, my dad told me he insisted on keeping the front porch light on day and night as a sign to me that I was welcome home.

However, I was out in the world, trying to feel alive, to be loved. Unfortunately, I looked in all the wrong places. I was in a free-fall in that pit that I thought I'd left at home as I turned to drugs, alcohol, men–anywhere I thought I could both deaden the pain and find life. I found neither. Instead I found pregnancy, abortion, and later, rape.

Years later, I got married and we had a child. The last thing I wanted was for my son to grow up like I had. I thought church was the answer. What I didn't know was that a co-worker had been praying for us for a year. I knew she went to church, so I asked her where. She gave me directions and we showed up one Sunday morning.

As I stepped over the threshold of the tiny church, I felt something different there. It was like stepping out of that black pit and into the Light. The presence of the Holy Spirit was thick in the room. As the band began to play, tears began to stream down my face. The love I'd been looking for all those years, the One who'd loved me even in the pit, was there in that room.

The answer was much more than just going to church. It was in knowing Christ. The Lord completed the work He began when I was a little girl. My family and I have all asked Jesus to be our Lord and Savior, even my dad, who prayed to receive Him five days before he passed away. And I know we have a home in heaven where the porch light is always on.

ABOUT THE AUTHOR

Dorci Harris lives in the Southwestern U.S. with her husband of twenty-five years, and she has two grown sons. She began blogging devotions over five years ago at the nudge of a friend. Dorci loves spending time with her family and friends, relaxing at the beach, riding horses, and baking, preferably with chocolate.

To read more about Dorci, go to:
http://faithwriters.com/testimonies.php

THE OFFER

By Rachel Malcolm

The noise of the party drifted out of my consciousness. My mind swirled as I shivered in shock. I had been offered death, but I let it go.

Gripping the counter, I leaned into the mirror. My pale skin contrasted my dark and wild eyes as I felt my body tense. I squeezed my eyes shut and screamed from my gut, but my voice betrayed me, and there was only silence.

The night had been no different from many others. The same faces, the same blue haze of smoke suspended in the air. I'd felt that same excitement mixed with anxiety that I usually felt just before I took magic mushrooms.

I settled into a round, wicker chair and waited for the high. It never came. Instead, I found myself looking into the light, and then came the choice. Though I never heard an audible voice, the question reverberated deep within my soul. "Do you want to die?"

The offer held me spellbound, and I struggled internally. I couldn't understand my sudden indecisiveness—of course I wanted to die. I had fantasized about death every single day for months. Each night, I ran as if I were being chased, my feet hastening me through the oppressive darkness that brought me back to the ocean. Standing at the water's edge, as the wind tangled my hair, I would long to fill my lungs with the salty water.

With certainty, I felt that all I had to do was say, yes, and it would be over. My family, thinking I had unwittingly taken poisonous mushrooms, would be spared the horror of a loved one committing suicide. It would be an accident, just an accident.

But as much as I wanted to, I couldn't say yes. The intensity of the light faded, and I crumpled back into the chair. My heartbeat thudded like heavy footfalls in an empty attic.

"Is there a reason for my life?" I cried out.

The hope that dawned on me over the following weeks contradicted my past. Before, life seemed futile, but suddenly I started searching for the truth. There had to be a purpose for my life.

Fate intervened, or so it seemed, bringing me a person from my past. I remembered the happy families, the organ music, the bread and wine from my childhood church where Kevin led the singing.

Living on a small island, I had seen him occasionally over the years, but now our circles had merged once again. Kevin often entertained at dances and parties that I attended. He brought questions to my mind as he sang of pain, choices, and finding God. It all seemed so silly and trite. How could Jesus' death bring life? I knew the Bible stories inside out. In my youth, I'd memorized Scripture and listened to Bible stories on tape every night. But after my parents divorced, I had resolved that it was just a crutch. God didn't exist...or did he? I couldn't dismiss him anymore. Kevin's words held weight.

I also had realized that life without God was life without meaning. I went down that path, and it left me in a vacuum. I couldn't live a life that was devoid of eternity. And then there was that choice. Where had it come from? Who did it come from? Could there be a God after all?

Memories stirred in my mind, memories that I had chosen to forget. I remembered listening to Christian music in my childhood home. Sunlight danced on the mustard coloured rug, streaming in from the sliding glass door. I sang along with my whole heart and offered my life to God. Joy bursting within me, I ran outside. Climbing onto a solitary rock, I raised my arms to the Lord and rejoiced in the warmth of his love.

Weeks later, I sat at the feet of a Sunday school teacher with a dozen other children. "Who memorized their verse from last week?"

"Me! Me!" I raised my hand, waving it back and forth before spouting off the verse.

The teacher smiled; her eyes were kind and showed approval. She began the Bible story. I usually loved them, but this one made me uncomfortable and stirred up anger from within.

"Why did the shepherd have to look for the lamb?" the teacher asked us after the story. I was usually the first to raise my hand, but that day I hung back. The story of the lost sheep left me feeling betrayed.

Later that evening, I lay awake pondering why God had cared about the sheep that wandered away. After all, it was its own fault that it got lost. And why all the rejoicing when it was found? What about all the good sheep that never got lost, why wasn't there rejoicing over them? In my child-like exuberance I threw back the covers and crawled to the open window. I rested my chin on my arms as I took a deep breath. "I'll never leave you, Jesus."

So what brought me to a hopeless life of parties and drugs? The turning away didn't happen all at once, but looking back, I realized that it began with the hardening of my heart that day as I listened to the story of the lost lamb. I questioned God's goodness, and my own pride made me feel distant from God's love.

But now God was seeking me. It wasn't something that I questioned. I was the lost lamb, and I wanted to be found.

I was at Kevin's next performance and had come to love the sound of his voice. Riveted, I listened to the words interwoven with rich melodies from his guitar. His lyrics had depth because he knew God personally. I watched his fingers fly over the strings. Instead of one sound hole in the centre, his guitar had a series of small holes arching out from the fret board. Each opening was surrounded by overlapping leaves of different coloured wood. The design reminded me of angel's wings.

That evening we sat outside together. A gentle breeze wrapped us in the calming scent of cedar and made the bamboo leaves whisper. There was so much on my heart, and I showered Kevin with questions. "How did you become a Christian? What makes you believe there really is a God? How do you know if he is real?" My body slumped forward as I sighed. Tilting my head, our eyes met.

"Can God forgive me?"

Kevin rested his hand on my shoulder. "God wants you back, Rachel."

How could that be? Why would God love me after I had turned away, hurt others, and despised his gifts? But it was true! Now I understood that the Shepherd searched for his lost lamb because he is a God of mercy whose love never fails. Tears of gratitude flowed from my eyes and dripped from my chin as God's love flooded my heart.

I had been lost, but now I was found.

~ ~ ~

ABOUT THE AUTHOR

Rachel Malcolm lives in the bush in Northern British Columbia, Canada, with her husband and six children. She keeps busy with homeschooling and is currently illustrating a children's book. Desiring to encourage other moms, Rachel writes a blog called *Cherishing the Moment.*

To read more about Rachel, go to:
http://faithwriters.com/testimonies.php

THE PROMISE

By Lorraine Quirke

On March 18, 2004, I awoke when the sun peeked into my window, and I smelled leftover pizza and coffee on the dining room table. Fear hit me like a thunderbolt and crawled up my spine when I realized I had no place to go—I had lost my job the day before. A chill hung in the air and rattled my bones as I slid out of bed and moseyed into the living room. Meows sounded from around the couch and tears filled my glistening gray eyes. How long would I be able to pay for cat food or even pay the rent to keep from joining the ranks of the homeless? Adrenaline attacked my body until I received my first unemployment check. Now, I had to find a job.

Resumes flowed from my computer; calls to employment agencies and headhunters permeated the phone lines. I sweated out the year, but still believed I would find a job. A former boss and friends helped me research as I explored all possibilities. The preliminary interviews offered hope, and most of the time, human resources did call me for a second interview.

I picked up the phone with anticipation one day, only to hear the interviewer say, "I'm happy you are one of the two people we considered. The boss likes you and feels you are competent, but we hired the other person."

Blood drained from my face, a metallic taste filled my mouth, and my self-esteem slipped away. I kept trying, but again and again I heard the same things. A groan of fear flew over my lips. *Why won't anyone hire me? Why is it always someone else?*

The hope and belief God would find me a job plunged down a precipice. The rock on which I stood collapsed. Yet, I managed to cling to Jesus. He always provided me with inspiration, strength, encouragement, and love. I needed Him now desperately.

The security deposit paid my last month's rent, and I breathed a little easier when help arrived; my friend Ellen invited me to stay with her while I continued to look for a job. I moved in and put my furniture in storage. I wept as I watched my belongings loaded into a truck. How would I pay for it?

We struggled along for three months in her studio apartment. My back ached as I lay on a skimpy mattress on the floor while my cat stared and hissed at hers. One night, Ellen looked at me with glaring hazel eyes. "Please turn down the TV because I'm trying to read." All the normal irritants caused extra upset in a small apartment. Worry settled in the pit of my stomach.

One night, Ellen returned home and wanted to talk to me. She started, stopped, and finally spit out, "What are you going to do? I think you better have a Plan B. You can't stay here forever. I'll give you another month to find an alternative."

I studied her furrowed brow; she appeared angry, but I realized it was concern, so I touched her arm, saying, "I understand." My throat dried up, my body became mush, and I barely choked out the words, "There is no Plan B."

I shivered so much I had to get a sweater. Desperation wrapped around me like a shroud as I sought Him and His presence. *Where are you? I thought you loved me. Lord, what do I do now?* God showed me what I lacked; but would my trust cap fit?

Suddenly, Oklahoma flew into my mind. I discovered the Lord had a Plan B; He was sending me to Oklahoma to be a caregiver for my ninety-nine-year-old, gray-haired, frisky aunt. I rebelled; I couldn't believe God's plan would send me out of state. After my stomach settled, I became grateful I had a place to live.

The day before I departed from Chicago, I placed Honey in her carrier and dragged myself to Anti-Cruelty to give her back to them. Dejected, I left, hoping she would find a good home.

The next day, I arrived at the Oklahoma City airport with a large purse, suitcase, and garment bag. My brother greeted me saying, "Taking care of Aunt Gert hasn't been easy. I'm glad you're here."

When I grasped my blue suitcase, I had a menacing feeling.

Problems happened right away. Aunt Gert became upset, "Why won't this darn washing machine work? I'm not happy with the closets. It's too cold in here." I did the best I could for her.

During my first month in Oklahoma, I received a surprise in the mail. I opened a card, and a $100 check fell out for my monthly storage. A check, guided by angel wings, flew into my mailbox every month until I came back to Chicago. The Lord provided through Ellen again.

My journey into the unknown became the most stressful time I had ever experienced. I didn't know God's plan for my future. I prayed for help and strength. The sound of the crickets and the chirping of the Baltimore Oriole didn't ease my pain. Anxiety swept over me like tidal waves. What would happen next? Would I eventually go back to Chicago? Would I find a job?

A month later, Ellen called me with a surprise. "I found a cheap flight on Southwest and you leave for Chicago on July 3rd."

I jumped up and down, had some wine, and thanked God for His permission to go home. My aunt moved back with my brother; she would be fine with him.

After eleven months in Oklahoma, I boarded the plane, found a window seat, took a deep breath, and my spirit calmed for the first time in three years.

Arrival in Chicago excited me. I believed the stress would soon be over. Surprise!

The dream burst; I still couldn't find a job. Would this hell ever end? My goal of being a brave and faith-filled person eluded me, and anxiety filled my life.

When my mind flooded with thoughts of walking the streets and begging for money, I remembered Psalm 46:10, *"Be still and know that I am God." (NIV)* and whatever happened, He controlled my life. No matter what I feared, Jesus loved me; every time depression and fear hit, I received a shot of courage. But help would not be forthcoming until I reached out for an answer. Terror scrambled my brains, and my knees wobbled as I stepped out and dared to trust.

When I did reach out, I talked with the head of a homeless shelter.

"Wait, I have a great idea for you." She moved to her desk and searched for a flyer. "The YMCA has a new program and I think you would qualify." The program staff approved my application, and I moved into the YMCA.

A few months later while living at the Y, I turned sixty-two and started receiving Social Security, and I also found a part-time job. Because I had faith and obeyed His leading, I received four wonderful blessings: a program, a job, an apartment and a cat named Tiffie.

The Lord promises, *"I will never leave you nor forsake you."* *(Hebrews 13:5, NKJV)*

ABOUT THE AUTHOR

Lorraine Quirke is a retiree and new writer with a desire to bring Christians into a deeper faith. She is a member of ACFW and FaithWriters. She writes Christian fiction, articles, and animal stories for children. Lorraine resides in Illinois with her cat, Tiffie.

Read more by Lorraine:
http://faithwriters.com/testimonies.php

Unclenching My Fist

By Leigh Ann Reid

When my father walked out on us, I tried everything imaginable to fill the massive crater left in my soul. But what tools does an eight-year-old have? I scrambled. Early on, I made do with academic success, and later I sought approval from my classmates. But by middle school to fill the void in my heart, I settled into desperation for romantic relationships—throwing my body on the altar of whoever/whenever, sacrificing my dignity and self-esteem. I existed in a destructive, humiliating world of impurity and clung to every ounce of pseudo-love I gathered to fill the gaping emptiness.

During senior year, in the midst of this degrading ritual, one young man announced that he wanted to spend the rest of his life with me. Surely this was a permanent fill to the void! And I proceeded with the whitest wedding imaginable.

Within two years it was over. I filed for divorce.

Twenty-two, a college student, divorced, the hole in my heart had ragged edges. Disillusioned, distraught, and depressed, I started to rely on anxiety medications and began to drink. I started failing classes. I started to withdraw from my friends. The world started growing darker, faster.

To escape the ugly reality I was drowning in, I flew to the farthest place I could think of, Seattle, where my sister and her husband lived. I needed to run away, to gather myself, to mend my heart.

Alone in my sister's office, I exchanged angry words with my horrible-boyfriend-of-the-month. He slammed the phone down on me, and it slammed down on my life. I slid against the wall, down into a heap on the floor, gasping for breath.

I realized how far gone I really was. Divorced. Abused. Used. A failure with a disastrous past and no future. My existence was hopeless. The walls had finally caved in.

It's hard to explain exactly what happened in that moment because it's so far outside the realm of typical human experience. But in that instant, crumpled on the floor, without praying or asking for God's help in the absolute darkest moment of my life, I felt the presence of Jesus in the form of a hand gently laid on my shoulder.

Instantly I knew it was Him, and His presence alone gave me an unexpected, overwhelming sense of peace. In that darkness, hope suddenly shone. His presence told me that my life meant something. That it was redeemable. That I was loved. Most importantly I immediately felt forgiveness for years of sinful decisions I had made. I knew I would never be the same.

I immediately went home and started sharing what had happened with anyone who would listen. I got a personalized license plate on my car that said: "Jesus Freak." I visited churches. I devoured Scripture with a hunger I couldn't explain. I knew from my experience how real Jesus was, and I wanted to know Him intimately.

In almost every regard, I was changed. Almost. And I started to live as if it meant I were no longer vulnerable. My roots were taking hold, but they were shallow. Soon I found myself frequenting my same old habits and surroundings, my Christian-fish-emblazoned car taking me there. I began to live a strange, dual life, clinging to sin that was so comfortable.

And when conviction came I'd repent and turn back. I lived this confusing cycle over and over. Why was this happening? I thought the experience I'd had with Jesus meant I was bigger than temptation, stronger than failure. In my baby faith I didn't yet know that an experience with Jesus is not what overcomes the worldliness in us; it is Jesus alone.

I had many hard lessons still to learn. Five months into my new life as a Christian I got pregnant. Looking back on how I was living, I imagine it was inevitable. In the blur of many days and nights gone wrong, it had only taken one night of believing I was strong enough to handle a drink with some friends at the bar. And then another. And another.

I have forgiveness now. If this goes badly, I'll just repent in the morning and start over again. But this cheap faith I was living with had consequences, and they were real.

When the reality of my situation sunk in, all I cared about was finding a way out. I refused to consider the options as I leaned on the excuse of wanting to protect God's reputation, as he needed me to protect his good name. In truth, it was a tragic combination of pride, fear, and shame. I drove myself, alone, to an abortion clinic a town away, and there I endured what I can only describe as the most horrible, heart-wrenching, emotionally detestable experience of my life.

I remember sitting in the recovery room, disgusted with myself, contemplating the horror and selfishness of what I had just done. I remember looking around me, dumfounded that I was even there. I thought as a Christian, my life had been redeemed. I thought I was empowered. *God, if it was really you in that room in Seattle, where are you now? Why would you allow this? I thought you were a healer? I thought you saved people? Why?*

In a clear and gentle voice, over my tears, God answered me. "Leigh-Ann, I love you. I came to redeem your life and do something amazing with it...for my glory, not yours. If you want the life of abundance I have promised, you have to give me your life. All of it. I can't make it beautiful while it's clenched in your fist. This is as far as you get in your own power. This disgusting place is as far as you get. Give it to me. And I will give it back to you, redeemed."

There, in that moment is where my real life in Christ began. I left my brokenness and much of the rest of myself there...my old life, my old habits. His love was the only solution to the aching void, and now I knew it.

I was going to give Him everything. It would take time and the development of my faith to do it, but it would become the purpose of my life.

It is when we unclench our fists and hand over our lives that we receive our lives. It's only in our humility that his power can fully be demonstrated. Are you broken? Have you unclenched your fists and put your life in his hands? Have you given him the opportunity to do miraculous things with the shattered pieces of yourself, rather than clinging to them, burying them, disguising them?

I challenge you to release your grip and let go. Because when you, do your life—the one you are longing for—will truly begin.

ABOUT THE AUTHOR

Leigh-Ann Reid is the wife of an active-duty Marine Officer and a homeschooling mom of three. Currently residing in Tampa, Florida, the fifth duty station in twelve years, she embraces the life of a military "nomad," a special calling by which she has been able to minister and serve those who serve. Leigh-Ann's other passion is helping women come to a deeper understanding of Christ's love for them and helping them mobilize for his Kingdom.

Read more from Leigh Ann Reid:
http://faithwriters.com/testimonies.php

UNEXPECTED

By Joanne Sher

"Hi. It's Charley."

I smiled. It was the religion editor, hopefully with an assignment.

"Hey, Charley! What's up?"

"I need a story covered on Saturday for Sunday's paper. A Christian woman's conference. I figured you could be objective."

Charley was right. As a Jew, I'd approach it with skepticism. Fake, mushy women screaming "Hallelujah" and praising God for their wonderful lives. Plus a story in the Sunday paper? Not common for me.

This could be fun.

"Sure. What do I need to know?

***

Saturday morning, I grabbed my reporter's notebook and press pass, kissed my husband Marc goodbye, then drove off.

I'd be bored within minutes. Thankfully, I had to return to the newsroom by noon—otherwise I'd be listening to Jesus stuff even longer.

I parked by the newspaper office and strolled two blocks to the venue. I'd pick a section of the arena to ask several people why they came, what they thought, etc.

By the time I found a spot in an aisle, the first presenter was speaking. I scanned the attendees while listening for anything interesting from the stage.

Surprisingly, the 10,000-seat arena was nearly full. Though I didn't recognize the speakers, their tone and sincerity, their smiles and words, seemed authentic – worth listening to. Not what I expected.

A few rows down, a woman in her early thirties sat with a girl who looked around ten. The woman nodded at the presenter every minute or so, and the girl smiled, her chin in her hand. I approached them, asking if they'd do an interview. They agreed, so we spoke between presenters.

Whenever my subjects were engaged with the speakers, I looked around me. I didn't just see people. I saw a camaraderie, a closeness, a peace: women smiling, whispering at one another, acting like family.

These women couldn't know each other personally. Yet I felt a sisterhood, a connection among them as they listened and participated. The shocker? I also felt like part of it.

I wanted to sit to listen to the music, the speakers, the women in the arena, and soak it up. I was intrigued by what I saw and felt. Writing this article no longer seemed important. I wanted to stay, to learn more and to marinate in the experience.

I glanced at my watch and sighed. This story needed to be written and ready to go in the next hour and a half.

After gathering a few more quotes, I left. Thoughts were salsa dancing in my brain, but they weren't about the article. I loved this sensation. I didn't want it to end.

Moments later I was on the street. Despite my wish, I was empty. That feeling had left and I felt hollow.

But I couldn't think about that. I needed to write a coherent article. So I forced my brain to focus on the notes I'd taken. I read them over as I walked to the newspaper office, and again at the computer as I composed my story. But I couldn't keep those thoughts away. Still, I filed my story, drove home, and told Marc about my day.

My practical husband asked a very practical question. "What are you going to do about it?"

Part of me wanted to learn about Christianity. I had so little knowledge. Yet I'd heard countless negative things about Jesus in my growing-up years.

I decided to start with my roots: Judaism.

I checked our bookcases and saw *The Sacred Writings* collection. Each book in the series included the texts of a different major religion. I pulled out *Judaism: The Tanakh.*

I sat, pen and sticky notes beside me, and turned to Genesis.

"In the beginning..."

***

I closed the book, placing it on the table.

In the past few days, I'd read Genesis through Joshua, amazed at how much I'd never read before, and at my reaction.

I booted up my computer, opened a document and scrolled to the end—I'd typed four pages of ponderings already. I added more thoughts, contemplating the endless battles and bloodshed.

More questions.

I didn't know what to think, but I knew I needed to keep reading.

***

"One down; one to go."

I returned *The Tanakh* to the bookcase. My next reading material rested beside it, but I left it there. I bit my lip and considered what I'd just finished.

The last two weeks, I'd devoured every word, typing sixteen single-spaced pages of reflections, questions, and observations.

With both excitement and anxiety, I pondered the next step. I didn't know what I would find, but I remembered my friend Chip's statement about my difficulties with some Old Testament issues.

"Most of what disturbs you in the Old Testament will thrill you in the New."

So I pulled out my *Sacred Writings* book of Christian scriptures and turned to Matthew's Gospel.

***

After six days and eight more pages of notes, I finished the New Testament. The past three weeks had been the most intense I'd ever experienced.

Christ's words captivated me. Paul's letters, and his testimony, fascinated. And it applied to me. Chip was right: many of my issues with the Old Testament were addressed in the New, and what I learned *did* thrill me.

Wanting to be like Jesus made perfect sense. Even *I* wanted to be like Him.

Yet, accepting Him as divine went against my most basic beliefs.

The center of Judaism, and the prayer every Jew knows by heart, is Deuteronomy 6:4: the Shema:

"Hear, O Israel: The LORD our God, the LORD is one."

God is one. How could Jesus be God? How could the Trinity be one as the Shema says?

I needed more answers. To attend a church. To talk to Chip. Read the Bible again.

But first, I needed to go through my notes and process them.

***

Shortly thereafter, I went to church.

It wasn't what I expected. There wasn't a prayer book or a Bible—just a songbook. They brought their own Bibles. We sang a lot, but nothing familiar to me. The songs were nice, though.

What surprised me most was the sermon. It was relevant to my life, and to the real world. There was no exposition of a Scripture passage or story without an application.

I also started rereading the Bible from the beginning. I'd never been as engrossed in anything as I was in God.

***

Four months after I finished my initial read-through, it all clicked. During my morning Scripture reading, I got to a passage I had read before—but this time I saw it with new eyes.

But he was pierced for our transgressions, he was crushed for our iniquities; the punishment that brought us peace was upon him, and by his wounds we are healed. We all, like sheep, have gone astray, each of us has turned to our own way; and the LORD has laid on him the iniquity of us all. (Isaiah 53:5-6 NIV)

Right in the book of Isaiah, Christ was described more clearly than in many New Testament passages. By His wounds I am healed. The Lord laid on Him our iniquity. He wore the punishment that brought *US* peace.

How could I not accept Jesus as my Messiah?

ABOUT THE AUTHOR

Joanne Sher is a Jew by birth, a Christian by rebirth, and a writer by gift. A native Southern Californian, she now lives happily in West Michigan with her husband and two school-aged children. She loves writing for children, and is a regular blogger at her own site and the FaithWriters blog (www.faithwriters.com/blog).

See samples of her writing here:
http://faithwriters.com/testimonies.php

TRIALS AND TRIUMPHS

FAITH UNDER FIRE

A TRIPLE DOSE OF GRACE

By Chris Goglin

The diagnosis was in–Stage IV colon cancer–incurable. No hope.

My eighty-six-year-old dad had been healthy all of his life, yet with a verdict from the doctor, life instantly became a priority. Our extended family and friends had fervently prayed for years that Dad would develop a personal relationship with God. We all had, but to no avail. He was a stubborn man.

On March 12, 1949, Mom surprised Dad with the birth of twin girls, appropriately born on his birthday. Consequently, the three of us faithfully celebrated our unique birthdays together every year. Mom, my twin sister, Linda, and I accepted Jesus within a year of each other, but Dad would not let *religion* affect his life.

"You women go to church," he grumbled, "but don't try to talk me into it!"

He was the head of the household, and three women could not tell him what to believe!

Many times I had nervously approached him in his worn-out recliner by the TV, where he smoked his pipe, watched football.

"Who's winning?" I said, trying to encourage a response. "Would you like a ham sandwich?"

It was difficult for me to speak to Dad. He was *always* right, and I felt so unworthy to communicate with him on any level.

"The Browns are losing again...not much of a game...Yeah... bring me a sandwich."

"OK. I'll be right back." I squeamishly grinned and kicked myself for chickening out again.

This had been our conversation for years. It was polite. It was simple. It was not the loving dialog between a father and daughter

I'd always hoped for.

A married woman now, I deserved a little more respect, I thought. It was not until Dad was sitting in that same chair many years later—after receiving the diagnosis of cancer—that I bravely blurted out my intentions.

"Dad, could I talk to you about something? Would it offend you if I talked about God?"

He looked up from watching *The Price is Right*. He gazed into my eyes, and I felt like a little girl again waiting for her punishment.

"No, it wouldn't offend me." He muted the TV. "I know what you are going to say, and this is NOT the right time."

I sighed and reluctantly obeyed, disappearing into the kitchen to retrieve his lunch.

The next day, we took Dad to the hospital for colostomy surgery. I helped him onto the narrow gurney that transported him to the operating room. I noticed his stomach protruding under his gown. He could no longer hide the cancerous tumor growing around his liver.

"Hey kiddo, do you think it will be a girl or a boy?"

I sadly smiled and boldly asked him if I could pray. To my amazement, he held out his hand.

"Dear Lord, please be with Dad on his journey of recovery, and help him to know that you love him."

Dad looked up, but did not utter a word. He was a proud man.

I watched him as the nurse swiftly wheeled him down the long corridor to the operating room, and I trusted God to take over from there.

When Linda and I arrived at the hospital the next morning, Dad was in terrible pain, spitting up black mucous. My hand touched his forehead, and he awakened briefly and looked into my eyes.

"I LOVE JESUS!" Dad firmly said and abruptly drifted off to sleep.

Linda and I froze in amazement.

"Is he delirious? What did he say?" Had our dad realized the truth in the prayer I had said, or was he just saying what he knew we wanted to hear?

Excited, yet worried, I stood by his bedside for the next several hours. The powerful painkillers dripping through his IV turned him into a stranger. He was continually pulling at his bed sheets, not realizing we were there at all. Had we lost him already?

"Chrissie, do this...no...not that...listen to me!" Dad protested.

My sister and I both went along with his demands, but inside, we yearned for a familiar conversation. His angry outbursts continued for hours until he finally calmed down. Linda and I decided to pray around his bed, and just like before, he promptly emerged from his delirium.

"I was just talking to God."

Hastily I whispered, "What did you say to Him?"

"I told Him I loved Him!" Dad began to cry.

You can imagine the tears shed in that hospital room that day. God had blessed us with another sign of His grace. We were sure *this time* that he had accepted the Lord as his Savior.

What seemed a grueling tug of war with Satan, Dad once again became incoherent. I sat by his bedside, the beeping of the monitor lulling me to sleep. He awakened occasionally; he grabbed my arm thinking it was a calculator and became angry and confused.

I was emotionally exhausted when Dad saw me crying by his bedside. Miraculously, he responded again. He reached for my hand. I jumped, expecting a scolding.

"It's OK. Just let it all out," he said. "Do you know how to get to Heaven?"

Through my tears, I said, "Yes, do you know?"

Dad paused and blurted out triumphantly, "Jesus Christ!"

I passionately squeezed his hand. God had given us another sign that He was in control. Several more days passed with continued disorientation. Then again, as if God had waved his magic wand, my silver-haired father was sitting up in bed.

"He ate his breakfast this morning," an orderly remarked, "and is much more responsive today."

Trying to sort out the ups and downs of my emotions, I noticed a change in Dad.

"Hey," he almost shouted, "what's with the small TV on my wall? It doesn't compare with my fourty-one-inch."

So happy he was back, I ignored past traumas and reminisced about good times all afternoon. I lifted his hand to say good-bye, and he suddenly pulled it close and squeezed it with an extraordinary firmness. I'll never forget it, because he never did this before, unless he was angry. I felt he knew something we did not. It was as if through the firmness of his hand, he was apologizing for all the time we had missed and how much he loved me.

The phone rang the next morning, and the nurse from the hospital urged us to get there immediately. We approached his room, fearful of what we might see. Dad was lying on his side, struggling to breathe. Mom and Linda held his hands, and I ran my fingers through his soft white hair.

"We are here Dad, it's OK. You will be with Jesus soon."

We all read the 23rd Psalm together. His eyes suddenly opened wide in surprise and seemed to want to tell us something wonderful. Did he see Jesus? Were there angels around us? We didn't know.

He slowly closed his eyes, as if to say, "It's finally over, I'm home."

We reluctantly left his room, looking back one more time at a lifeless body. We may have closed the door on Dad's life on earth that day, but God opened our hearts to the miracle of salvation, and our grief turned to joy.

ABOUT THE AUTHOR

Chris lives with her husband, Rich, in Cottonwood, Arizona. They have five loving children and five grandchildren. Chris has published with David C. Cook, Standard Publishing and the Christian Communicator newsletter in the past and has served as editor/publisher for her church newsletter. She is currently an administrative assistant.

You can learn more about this author at:
http://faithwriters.com/testimonies.php

Accepting Suffering from His Hand

By Andrea Van Ye

The concrete beneath our feet in the open-air parking structure cracked eerie moans, and we walked carefully towards the hospital doors. It wasn't just cold that afternoon, it was frigid, as only a January day in Wisconsin can feel. The sharp wind cut across our faces; confusion and uncertainty cut across our hearts. The only thing we smelled was frozen fragments of air—and fear.

I was thirty-one-weeks pregnant. Without warning, I went from enjoying my pregnancy to worrying about what was happening: nine weeks too soon for my baby to be born, and my water broke, or rather, trickled. Shortly there after, labor ensued.

After a long night of medications and monitoring, labor subsided, and I was placed on bed rest with hopes of making it three more weeks. But I didn't. One week later, my uterus became infected, and fevers raged and my body ached. Under duress our baby boy was born.

He arrived into the world blue and quiet. We cried. The doctors wrapped him in a blanket, swooped him by my face so I could see his, and then disappeared through the doors, carrying a piece of my heart. They ran him to the NICU.

He survived, although quite sick, with tubes and ticking machines helping to sustain his life. We went home empty-handed. I sat on the stairs of our small home and bellowed out to the Lord, "It wasn't supposed to be this way."

As the weeks went by, our son grew gradually stronger, learned to breathe, learned to suck, learned to swallow on his own. Tubes and ticking machines were removed and taken away. And then one day, the doctors proclaimed that his prognosis was great. He would do just fine, and we were allowed to take him home.

God was good.

Our son's time at home was unexpectedly challenging. He was on a monitor, and he was extremely fussy. Nothing settled him, but we were grateful for his life.

It never crossed our minds that there was something wrong.

Seven months later—this time on a warm sunny day—we walked through the same parking ramp for a routine appointment at the Premature Baby Clinic.

Professionals met with us. They examined our son from head to toe and poked and prodded our ears with questions and more questions. It didn't take long for me realize that we were answering "no" to questions that should be "yes" and "yes" to questions that should be "no."

And then, in one final, blunt statement from the doctor, our hearts imploded, along with our dreams.

"Your son has Cerebral Palsy. We can't tell if he'll ever walk or talk or eat on his own. Go on home, and we'll be in touch soon." If anything was said after that, we didn't hear it. Our ears were numb, as numb as our hearts.

That evening, we walked in the door of our pastor's home and fell into his arms and the arms of his wife. "We are scared and hurting so deeply. We don't know how to do this. How are we ever going to make it? How do we trust Jesus in all of this? It wasn't supposed to be this way."

We sobbed. Our bodies shook and our hearts shattered. Uncertainty and sorrow settled into our family story.

Our pastor and his wife held us on their couch and cried. They listened to us and prayed with us, and then they gave us the most valuable gift they could give our souls. They gave us perspective, a bigger perspective: God's perspective.

"We know this is very hard, but here is what you must do: accept this from the hand of God. Nothing slips through the His hand. He loves you, and He loves your son. Unfailingly."

They gave us truth that gave us hope, and the Lord continued to use that truth time and time again.

For nineteen years we walked through doctor appointments, surgeries, therapies, social-and-emotional struggles, and more. For nineteen years we experienced victories and joys, too. For nineteen years, we accepted life as it came from the Hand of God.

It hasn't always been easy, nor is it now.

We continually live in the tension between God's goodness and His will for our lives and for the life of our son.

Each day, our son struggles in one way or another. He is a young adult, trying to come to an understanding of who he is. He struggles with what God has for Him and who God is to Him, and probably, most of all, why a loving God asks Him to carry this burden.

We struggle, too.

Many times, when uncertainty about the present and the future cuts across my heart, again, like on that frigid winter day, I cry out to the Lord, "It wasn't supposed to be this way." It is then that He brings my mind back to the visit on the pastor's couch, and I remember God's hand.

Sometimes, the Lord hands us something that does not look like love. It looks like pain and difficulty and uncertainty and loneliness and hardship and heartache—but it is love. Not love, as the world measures love, but only as God measures love. It is not to harm us or pain us, but to grow us and to show us that Jesus, who suffered for our sake, is all we truly need.

Over the years, I've increasingly realized that when the Lord gives us something hard, He does not hand it over and leave it to our care.

He holds the suffering—and us—in His hand, and He gives us more.

He gives more hope. He gives us the ability to accept His will. He gives us comfort. He leads us and directs us in the way we should go. He gives the strength and the wisdom to help us in our sorrow. He provides peace, and He offers us rest in the palm of His hand.

Throughout the years and in the tomorrows that follow, we may never understand why the Lord has handed us this particular burden to carry. I don't always like what it looks like, but He knows what is best. He holds everything. Nothing slips from His hand. He is on His throne. He directs all things for His eternal purposes, and He never fails. Nor does His love.

It is true, and it is comforting. In trials and tensions and tear-drenched difficulties, God has a loving purpose and plan, handed to us in the palm of His hand for our good and for His glory.

ABOUT THE AUTHOR

Andrea Van Ye lives with her husband and five children in Neenah, Wisconsin. Andrea's passion is to bring hope and encouragement through God's truths. She writes and speaks at women's Bible studies and is involved in Women's ministry at her local church.

You can learn more about this author at:
http://faithwriters.com/testimonies.php

BROKEN-HEARTED WHOLENESS

By Frankie Kemp

I was an eleven year old girl when I knew I had to have Jesus and that He had something to offer me that I was desperately missing in my life. Jesus gave me the most real moment I had ever experienced. That day definitely changed my heart, but it was only the beginning. All my life, He has been teaching me that He is the road, the light ahead, and the quiet rest. He is the home of my soul.

God is good. His mercy, grace, and constancy–revealed to me through Jesus–are the strength of my heart, but this life is not always pretty, and it definitely has not always turned out according to my plans. Even though I would never ask to have hardship, pain, or sorrow, I now praise God for these things because those are the exact times when He plucked me from the ground and cradled me in His arms. The circumstances that I cannot change have compelled me to fall prostrate before Him, and confront the fact that I have a constant need to be solidified and grounded in the truth about who He is, and what He wants for me and from me. I have to admit that I have learned to see Him best when I need Him the most. I know that I have been surrounded by His grace my entire life, but I hadn't always understood exactly what that meant.

I have only begun to grasp the depth of His love for me in the wake of feeling completely unloved and totally useless. I have thrown more than one all-out, screaming, snotty two-year-old fit in the most holy place ever—the quiet places of my heart where it is impossible to be anyone but me, even though I am in the presence of the Spirit of the Living God whose holiness I can barely comprehend. He has mercy on me there, teaching me to know what grace looks like. I used to depend on certain things like happiness, answers to prayers, and a sense of peace to prove that God loved me. When some parts of my life fell apart, God taught me, that even in the midst of destruction; He still had a plan to show me His everlasting, unconditional love.

Three years ago, my marriage crumbled, and my version of my family fell apart. So did I. I like to think that I am good at pretending to hold it all together in front of the watching world, but inside I was a mess. My heart was a hurricane of hurt and full of questions. There were days upon days when I wanted nothing more than to stay in bed and sleep until the storm died, or until I was "normal" again. Praise God that His grace and purpose are bigger than my emotions, my understanding, and my foolish, fallen nature. He has always been perfect at drawing the truth from me and encouraging me to seek and accept the truth from Him.

The break-down days were the worst days, but also the best days. I would cry, *"Lord, where are you? Do you SEE what is happening? Why do I feel like you have forgotten all about me? This isn't supposed to be happening to me, is it? I cannot face another day if I feel like you have rejected me, too."* He never rejected me, but the hunger for Him forced me to question Him. I had to know that He hadn't forgotten me, so that I could face my life. In my quest, I had to devour Scripture.

Through these days, God taught me, for the majority of my journey with Him, what I have asked of Him most often is permission to be the one in charge of everything, even my relationship with Him. I thought I was honoring God by working hard to do what I could never do. I couldn't change the biggest problems in me, but I was still trying, praying, and going to church while wanting to be in control of everything. I had completely forgotten all that God had given me by Grace and through faith in Christ. No wonder I fell apart when things fell apart all around me. No wonder I blamed myself for every bad thing that had ever happened. No wonder I could not feel God's love for me.

God did not redeem my broken marriage. He did not make my sons compliant, always ready to obey me without question. He didn't turn me into the super-woman I believed I should be. He did not instantly rebuild all the inevitable piles of rubble that come when a household that is built on shifting sand comes crashing down. Instead, He revealed the cornerstone of my heart, so that I could see that He has always been the builder and giver of good gifts. I needed better eyesight—eyesight that is a gift of grace.

When I cried out in my despair because I did not feel loved, God heard my cries. I poured out my hurt in ink on tear-stained paper, and He responded. He didn't work by changing my circumstances, but by leading me to remember my Savior. He showed me everything that He did for me when He gave me eyes to recognize Jesus. Every time my pride accused Him or tried to justify me, the Spirit drew me to the truth. He also used His people to take care of many of my daily needs. Even when I was too proud to ask for help, He did not leave me to myself or give me temporary solace. Instead, He gave me Himself, showing me that He has always been there— which is exceedingly, abundantly MORE than what I was asking, and definitely more than I ever could have earned or deserved.

His grace has taught me that it is only deep trust in Him that enables me to find comfort in shame and loss. I cannot muster this kind of trust on my own. It either comes as a gift in the immediate moment, or the gift is revealed in me through the struggles of this life that drive me to my knees. It is there that I seek Grace and Mercy, the beautiful seeds of Faith and Hope. Either way, I get to see Him. He's shown me His sweetest promises when I have tasted what it is to desperately need to believe them. I have to admit that sometimes Grace looks like waiting for more. Sometimes, it looks like falling into His Word because that is exactly where I want and need to go.

God continues to break my heart so that He can heal my heart. This is why Grace is so beautiful, so amazing, and so true. His presence in my life has taught me that on those dark days when I find myself wrestling to get my bearings, my best option is to be still, always waiting and looking for the Light, and to know that He is God. I now understand what it is to be glad, even when I do not like my circumstances. It is a comfort to remember that He does not depend upon my ability to see and understand what He is doing in the moment to accomplish His purposes. What a lovely rest! I would not trade this. I now know, up close and personally, that He commands every hurricane. This is the hope of the broken-hearted. His name is Jesus.

ABOUT THE AUTHOR
Frankie Kemp lives and teaches high school English in Jessieville, Arkansas. As a life-long learner herself, she is finding a new joy in being taught to use her love for writing to point to the most beautiful message of all, Jesus.

Read more from Frankie:
http://faithwriters.com/testimonies.php

BUILT ON THE ROCK

By JoAnne E. Billison

I'll never forget the morning my husband voiced his objections to my new-found faith. With furrowed brow and tightly pressed lips he threw a kitchen towel across the counter. "You have to stop going to church!"

He continued his outburst with statements like, "I don't know who you are anymore, but you're not the woman I married." And, "If you keep going to church, our marriage will end!"

Shock quickly set in and I began to tremble. I didn't know how to respond to his rage, but somehow managed to say, "I'm sorry, I can't stop going...I need God in my life." I tried to explain that I could manage both church and our marriage, but my words were like tiny pebbles that bounced off his chest and fell to the floor. Nothing penetrated his heart that morning. He barked objections over my new relationship with Jesus until he had nothing left to say. Then, he left me standing alone in the kitchen, numb and afraid.

Being married and mother of two made living out my new faith very challenging. I was caught completely off guard when my husband tossed the towel across the counter. His protest shook me to the core of my being. Our "discussion" that morning became the first of many. Sadly, for the next ten years our marriage eroded, and along with it, my emotional well-being.

My husband never physically left our home, but he emotionally left our marriage. Overnight I became a single parent living in a hostile environment. In the blink of an eye, my new-found faith was tested. I wasn't sure what to do. I didn't know whether I could believe the Scriptures and promises of God—or not?

What I really wanted to know that fretful day was *can I trust*

God? I knew He was the Creator of the Universe and Sovereign over all things, but did He care about me personally?

My circumstances left me with two choices; embrace my faith and live boldly for Christ, or quit going to church and utilize my own strength to fix my marriage...if possible.

I chose to believe God. I decided that if my faith was to grow, I had to push beyond a simple belief in the existence of God and move into a faith that was grounded in the promises and attributes of God. I chose to accept everything I learned about God as *true*. He is our Sovereign God and He cares for me deeply.

Now came the hard part—releasing control over my marriage. In prayer, I told God I would trust Him with my situation no matter what happened next. I gave him complete power over it and chose to live one day at a time. I felt like Abraham leaving behind all familiarity (Genesis 12). I walked forward and found myself journeying in a foreign desert.

Trusting God meant I had to let go of my expectations. I had to let go of my desire to see my husband beg for my forgiveness, and I had let go of the timeframe I believed things should resolve within my situation. God doesn't see time the way we do, so I had to learn patience. I learned to accept whatever He chose to bring or allow in my life. I faced a lot of disappointment. I bit my tongue and remained silent on more than one occasion. I lost my cool, made a few mistakes, and usually hated my circumstances because I was lonely, hurting and confused. Years passed by and I never saw any changes in my marriage. I just clung to Jesus and learned to endure.

No matter what I faced, God kept me moving forward. Somewhere in the midst of all the chaos, I began to recognize the feeling of his presence within me. That gave me a tremendous amount of peace. Experiencing his peace changed my perspective on everything. I stopped asking God to simply get me through my difficult marriage and began asking him to teach me from it. I decided to step out on a limb and take a look into my heart. As a result, I drew closer to God, closer than I ever thought possible.

One thing is certain, if we want to glimpse our own hearts, then our hardships are a road that'll take us there. As my heart opened before my eyes, I learned how controlling, selfish, judgmental, fearful and insecure I really am. Every time I prayed for God to work on my husband, he worked on me instead. God used my marriage as a tool to purify my heart and shape me into a more Christ-like person. This was not easy, by any means. It was the hardest thing I ever experienced. In fact, some days felt like sandpaper was rubbing the skin right off my bones. I was humbled for sure, but I also discovered the true meaning of forgiveness. I came to appreciate Jesus and the cross much more deeply. I understood grace in a very personal way. The process taught me to give grace to my husband because God so lovingly poured it out on me.

What I went through was hard, but not all bad. I had a few good days too. Sometimes the joy God poured into my heart was so overwhelming, I couldn't breathe! Many times I saw the fingerprints of God surround an amazing outcome to a difficult encounter. I watched my boys grow up and embrace their faith in Jesus Christ and many old wounds were healed. The greatest gift I received from God throughout my ordeal was the privilege of witnessing my husband's heart slowly soften and grow loving towards me once again. God's ways are hard but they alone produce the best possible outcomes.

Suffering is a part of life in this world. I chose to face my hardship by trusting God and resolving my situation his way. I did this because more than anything else, I want my life to glorify and honor him.

The dark years of my marriage were scary, but in the end, they served me well. I grew strong and courageous. I gained inner peace and balance. I developed problem-solving skills and boundaries. I grew in character, integrity and so much more. I know trusting God with my situation *changed me* for the better.

God has worked wonders in my husband's heart, but he still does not share my faith. My marriage is still complicated. But Jesus tells us that when we build our lives on the rock, meaning by his commands and teachings, we can weather any storm (Matthew 7:24-27).

I believe this wholeheartedly. Because of what I've been through, I know without a doubt, God can be trusted with my marriage, and with my life.

ABOUT THE AUTHOR

JoAnne lives in the United States and has been involved in ministry for over a decade. She received her MDiv degree in 2009 and is the author of Walk Free: *An Uncommon Cure for the Common Heart.* It is her heartfelt prayer that her story inspires followers of Christ to deepen their faith, trust God, and face difficult life situations with renewed hope.

You can read more about JoAnne at:
http://faithwriters.com/testimonies.php

CHRISTMAS ANGELS

By Leola Ogle

"Help me! I can't do this anymore. I can't." I hiss the strangled words into the air to no one—to anyone. Although the words are a whisper, inside they are a screaming rage. Emotional exhaustion permeates my being, stealing my energy like a ravaging beast. I am not old, yet I stumble down the narrow hallway like an ancient, decrepit woman. I purposely avoid looking at the dismal, sparsely decorated Christmas tree in the corner of the living room. Why add to my gloom?

I open the door on the left, and seeing my two youngest daughters are asleep, I sigh in relief. By the suppressed giggling behind the next door, I know my two oldest daughters are awake. I lightly rap my knuckles against wood and mumble, "Knock it off and go to sleep. You have school tomorrow."

I wearily trudge back toward the living room.

My son calls out from the room addition that serves as his bedroom. "Mom, I need lunch money tomorrow."

"Okay. Go to sleep." I press my knuckles against my mouth to stifle the sobs that lie beneath the surface. I don't have lunch money. I don't have any money. We've lost our home, my dream house, the one at which we'd just had a pool built in the backyard. If not for dear friends who allowed us to live in this rental home, I don't know where we'd be.

"Why, God? Why?" I snatch my purse off the floor and dig through it for loose change. My finger pushes coins around the palm of my hand—a nickel short of enough for lunch money. I walk to my bedroom and search until I find five pennies.

Entering the living room again, I set the coins on the coffee table.

90

My eyes sweep over the tree with its small assortment of cheap gifts underneath. That hurts worse than anything. I rub my fingers across my forehead, and let the tears flow—quietly, lest I disturb my children.

I want to scream, stomp my feet like a toddler throwing a tantrum, pound my fists against the wall, fling curses into the air, and shake my fist at God. Instead, I curl into a ball on the sofa and cry until my blouse is wet. I accomplish nothing except a raging headache, and eyes swollen and raw.

I love God. I serve Him the best I know how. I'm involved in church, teaching classes, heading up the women ministry, always available for whatever task needs to be done. I remind God of this, as if He needs reminding. Do I hope to bargain with Him, impress Him, or shame Him into doing something?

I whisper my litany of complaints to God. How did I end up like this? My greatest downfall was dropping out of high school to get married. I just wanted to be a wife and mommy, an idealistic dream in the sixties. By the time I realized there wasn't going to be a happily-ever-after, I had brought five children into the world.

My life was on a downhill spiral, and I couldn't stop it. My marriage had gone from bad to worse, and I was struggling to maintain some semblance of normalcy while my husband was on the road. Now it was Christmas, and there wasn't money to buy gifts for my kids. Why must the kids and I suffer, for so many years, because of my husband's sins and lifestyle choices? He wasn't suffering; he was living like a single man driving a truck cross-country.

"God, please, please, please help us. It's Christmas. Christmas! I can't even scrape money together for school lunches, let alone good gifts. I am a mother, and this hurts." My tears start again as heaviness radiates from my chest to every part of my body.

Oh, I could whine about my plight to the dear saints at church, those who love me and my kids, and something would be done. But I am embarrassed to be broke again, to be the one in need. We have been helped so often.

I drift into an exhausted half-sleep, knees drawn to my chest, arms wrapped around myself to still my trembling. I awake with a start, jerking to an upright position as if pushed by an unseen hand. My eyes blink and focus on the twinkling lights of the Christmas tree. *Why am I sleeping on the sofa?* I wonder, before the ball of pain begins to build as a reminder.

I drop my head into my hands as a groan slips past my lips. *"Oh, God, I'm so sorry!"* Those few words contain the essence of my misery, but it goes deeper than that. I know God understands what I mean. I'm sorry for being mad at Him, sorry for whining, sorry for blaming Him for my problems.

From deep within, I know He's okay with my venting. He sees my heart, that it's not Him I'm mad at. I'm angry at my husband, at life, at my circumstances. I feel the sweet assurance that I am loved by God, that my children are more precious to Him than they are to me.

Standing, I look at the tree, at the motley assortment of cheap gifts. There are things more important, more valuable than gifts. We have each other, our health, a roof over our heads, and we aren't hungry. I inhale deeply and raise my hands heavenward in surrender to the One who spoke worlds into existence. In the chaos of my life, it is the hope I cling to.

I spin with my arms lifted high, a smile on my face. Whatever happens, I know that Jesus is moved with compassion by the cry of my mother-heart interceding on behalf of my children. I go to bed, reminding God of several people in the church who have finances and resources to bless us. *"Perhaps You can speak to someone's heart about us, God. But if not, we'll be okay,"* I say as I crawl into bed.

As He often does, God moves in a way that leaves no doubt the answer came from Him, and not from some finagling on our part. A group of radio and ham operators, part of a truckers' group, some-how learn of our plight. These Christmas angels arrive a few days before Christmas with more gifts than I can fit under our tree and groceries to last a few weeks. This rough-looking, rough-talking group sheepishly wave off our tears of gratitude.

More than thirty years later, it is a Christmas we still talk about. It wasn't the last of our struggles. There would still be times when I felt crushed beneath my circumstances, when I whined and railed at God. As I matured, the whining and railing seldom happened. God has always been faithful. Sometimes He delivered me from the circumstances, but more often, He held me up as I walked through them.

Through the hard times, I learned a deeper trust in God. I know He is God on the mountaintops, and God in the valleys. Because of His faithfulness to us, several of my children are in ministry today.

ABOUT THE AUTHOR

Leola Ogle lives in Phoenix, Arizona, USA. She and her husband, Jeff, are a blended family of eight children and many grandchildren. Their lives are filled with family times and church activities. Leola has been writing most of her life, but a few years ago decided to devote more time to the pursuit of a writing career.

Read more from Leola:
http://faithwriters.com/testimonies.php

EXCEPT GOD

By Allison Egley

"Who wants to accept Christ as Savior?" Over the next four days, I heard the Five Day Club leader ask that question, and I raised my hand. Finally, on the fifth day, the leader brought me aside, and I asked Jesus to be Lord of my life. I was only four at the time, but even then, I knew of my need for a Savior and wanted to place my trust in Him. Perhaps it was because I had already witnessed God work in my life, even if I wasn't able to recognize it as His work at the time. Little did I know then how much I would need to lean on God in the future. No one knew–except God.

Throughout my life, I have faced various medical trials. Although my mom's pregnancy and my birth were mostly uneventful, shortly after I was born, I stopped eating. No one really knows why–except God. I was tube-fed for a while until I finally started eating on my own again. I was also far behind in my physical development. Whether this and any of my other medical problems were related, no one knew–except God.

Fast-forward a few years to kindergarten, when at age six I had eye muscle surgery. It really wasn't a big deal, but as a kindergartner, I grew increasingly tired of explaining, for what seemed like the thousandth time, why I had a patch over one of my eyes.

Next I was placed on growth hormone therapy. I received injections of human growth hormone three to six times a week, which continued until adolescence. I was never diagnosed with growth hormone deficiency, but the doctors could find no other reason for my short stature. I was even part of a research group to determine whether growth hormone was effective for those not diagnosed with this deficiency. Why I was so short, no one knew–except God. As a child, I didn't care much that I was short, even when I was the oldest in the class and also the shortest. I trusted God, knowing He made me.

The next big medical event was when I was in third grade. I was sitting next to my mom in the doctor's office.

He turned to my mom. "You do realize your daughter's hips are out of the sockets, right?"

My mom looked to the doctor, and I looked to my mom with confusion.

The doctors discovered this while looking for something unrelated, and told us they had probably been that way for years. I never experienced pain, which surprised everyone–except God. Soon, I was scheduled for hip surgery. If I didn't have surgery then, my hips would likely have caused major problems by the time I was a teenager. Why my hips were out of their sockets, no one knew–except God. God gave me a special song to help me get through this time. The song was "Cares Chorus" by Kelly Willard, and it was on one of the "Psalty" tapes I listened to. It is based on I Peter 5:7 which says, *"...casting all your care upon Him, for He cares for you."* *(NKJV)*

On January 5, 1993, I had surgery to put both hips back in their sockets. For about six weeks after that, I was confined to a body cast. My legs were spread apart in a "V" shape. The cast covered both legs, continued past my hips, all the way to the bottom of my rib cage. I could not walk, stand, or even sit upright for those six weeks. That was a difficult time for me. Before the surgery, I remember feeling nervous. I loved school, and hated being away from the classroom and my friends. I wanted to see my friends at church, and at age nine, I certainly did not want to lie in bed all day. I thought about the faith I had first clung to at age four. I needed it then at age nine more than I ever had before. I also drew some of my strength from "Cares Chorus." The same God who knew then, and knows now, all the intricate parts of my body, the same God who knows exactly why I had those various medical problems, could give me strength. I could cast all of my worries, all of my fears and anxieties on Him. I didn't have to worry. This meant so much to me.

That doesn't mean I was never scared. I was afraid when the nurses wheeled me into the operating room. I was worried when I first started to learn to walk again after the cast was taken off. I was nervous when I returned to school after months of being away from my classmates, but I knew that God was in control. He would take care of me no matter what. If I didn't know what to do, He did.

About twenty years later, God brought another "except God" moment to my life. In January of 2010, I started having pain in my left hip. The pain started out minor, and I tried to ignore it. Due to my earlier problems, I wanted to pretend it wasn't happening. It soon developed to the point where I couldn't ignore it. On May 3, 2011, at age twenty-seven, I was diagnosed with severe arthritis of the left hip. No one expected that–except God. On February 13, 2013, I had a hip replacement. No one expected that I would need a hip replacement before I turned thirty–except God.

Once again, God brought "Cares Chorus" into my life, and I continued to cling to the promises of that song and I Peter 5:7. No one expected the same song to bring me such comfort twenty years later as I faced my second major hip operation–except God.

As an infant, one doctor told my parents he wasn't sure if I would live. Other doctors warned that I would have multiple disabilities, including learning disabilities. No one really knew my future–except God. I graduated from high school with a 4.1 GPA, and I graduated college summa cum laude. Though frequently sick as a child, I had perfect attendance for all four years of high school. No one expected that–except God.

At a young age, God tugged at my heart, causing me to eagerly raise my hand to follow Him. He's held my hand ever since. I don't know what God has in store for me in the future and what other "except God" moments I will experience, but I do know one thing. My God is a great God. No matter what, I know He's in control, and will give me the strength I need to step through life as He has each moment in my past. The same God who made the universe cares about me.

He sent a special song to a little girl, and that song has helped carry her throughout her life. No one expected that–except God.

~~~~~~~~~~~~~~~~~~~~~~~~~~~~~~~~~~~~

Author's Notes:
"Cares Chorus," Kelly Willard, Copyright 1978, Maranatha Praise, Inc.
I Peter 5:7 (NKJV)

ABOUT THE AUTHOR:
Allison Joy Egley lives in St. Peters, Missouri, USA. She works for the state department of Vocational Rehabilitation, an agency which helps people with disabilities find and maintain employment. In her free time, in addition to writing, she enjoy connecting with friends on the internet, helping in the church nursery, and getting involved in various musical productions at her church. She plans to keep writing as long as the Lord allows.

Read more from Allison:
http://faithwriters.com/testimonies.php

FROM FAILURE TO FAITH

By Barbara Caldwell

I will never forget the words of a campus psychiatrist, spoken in my last year of college, "Miss Caldwell," he said, "you are on the verge of a nervous breakdown. You'll have to withdraw from school and return at a later time."

Due to the fact that I was in my senior year, with only nine credits left to finish that summer, this news was the last thing I wanted to hear.

After going home and getting some rest, I thought this situation would be resolved quickly; unfortunately, my troubles were just beginning. Even though I didn't realize it at the time, I was headed for a long, hard journey.

Months after I arrived home, my doctor diagnosed me with Manic Depression, also known as Bipolar Disorder. I missed many enjoyable events because I was depressed, confused, or hospitalized. For nearly fifteen years, I was admitted to the hospital almost every year.

During that time, I suffered many heartaches and disappointments. I failed to obtain my college degree, and my marriage ended quickly. Severe stress prevented me from keeping a job. This, of course, added to my anxiety level. I even experienced brief times of homelessness. If not for God's protection, I wouldn't be alive today.

This illness almost destroyed me. During the depressed stage, I would isolate myself. I felt all alone, worthless, and embarrassed of having a mental health illness. My life seemed so hopeless, even though I struggled to see a ray of light. There were times when I would cry for no apparent reason. Sleep helped me to escape my problems, until I woke up, and then reality smacked me in the face.

The manic stage was just the opposite; I was bubbly, overconfident, and felt like I could conquer the world. During this period of the illness, I felt like there was nothing that I couldn't achieve. Whenever I experienced the manic episodes, I would travel to another state. Without my family and friends close by, I would find myself homeless until my mother found a way to bring me home. Without sufficient funds for food or shelter, I would leave with the clothes I was wearing. In the midst of all this, I felt like a complete failure. Soon, I would come to realize that idea was far from the truth.

Through all the ups and downs that I experienced, I realized that God had plans for me that differed from the ones I had in mind. God had allowed these things to happen to me in order to position me to do His perfect will. He used these negative experiences to shed a positive light. Second Corinthians 1:3-4 states, *"Blessed be God, even the Father of our Lord Jesus Christ, the Father of mercies, and the God of all comfort; Who comforteth us in all our tribulation, that we may be able to comfort them which are in any trouble, by the comfort wherewith we ourselves are comforted of God."(KJV)* This became my mission! After my last hospitalization in 1992, I did some soul-searching and praying as I had at other times. This time, however, was different. I asked God to heal me of the madness that troubled me, and then I totally surrendered my life to Him. At this point, I received a new mind and a new heart.

Amazingly, I now share the news of God's grace and His healing power. I haven't had an episode or hospitalization for nearly twenty-one years. I still take one medication, but I realize that the sole power of God has made the difference in my life.

God continues to use me, even now. I let others know that they can obtain the same victory in their lives. He is no respecter of persons. There is nothing too hard for Him! I've been led to a life of faith, and delivered from believing that I was a failure.

This illness has made me a better person, instead of a bitter one. It brings me great joy to encourage others. Sharing my misfortune, and my triumph from it, released me from the shackles of shame.

God has allowed me share the story of His love, grace, and healing power. He has used me through my writing, speaking, and singing. Since 2002, God has enabled me to write four books and complete several recordings.

I lost my degree and my husband, but I didn't lose Jesus. He promised to never leave me nor forsake me. This means more to me than anything. God is faithful; this fact gives me ever-increasing faith in Him.

I have no regrets concerning all I went through because I have been made a stronger person because of it. I may have failed in several areas of my life, but because of Christ, I am more than a conqueror!

ABOUT THE AUTHOR

Barbara Caldwell is the author of four Christian books; she has also written and recorded several songs. She lives in Georgia and cares for her elderly mother, while assisting her elderly aunt.

You can learn more about the author and read more of her work at: http://faithwriters.com/testimonies.php

"I'm Not Shaking; I'm Living in Peace"

By Sheila L. Mills

*"For our light affliction, which is but for a moment,
worketh for us a far more exceeding and eternal weight
of glory." 2 Corinthians 4:17 (KJV)*

While standing in line awaiting my turn to be submerged in the baptismal waters, I wondered if my embarrassing and uncontrollable hand tremors would overshadow this joyous occasion.

No way! This moment in time, my life was going to be different from all the others, including my childhood baptism. Just this once I wanted this to be a great life experience without people staring at me or asking the all-too-familiar question, "Your hands are trembling. Are you okay?"

I decided I would pray. "God, just this once, can you please give me 'still hands,' or am I asking for too much?"

I inched towards the baptismal pool, awaited God's answer, and thought back through the life challenges of my forty-seven years. I was born with hand tremors, caused by prenatal exposure to alcohol, stemming from my mother's alcoholism.

I've spent most of my childhood and adult life being ashamed of my hand tremors and wondering about God's purpose in allowing me to be born this way. Often, I wondered what earthly or heavenly good could possibly come out of the endless shame of never having hands that were *still* just for one moment.

I recalled the emotional imprisonment—feeling the need to constantly hide my hands, barely lifting my hands during praise and worship and not shaking hands with someone. I remembered the fear I felt at the dinner table when it was my turn to pass a dish. *What if I spilled the food?*

Even worse, I avoided holding hands during altar prayer to avoid the embarrassment of being asked, "Are you okay?"

As I got closer to the baptismal pool, I recalled the constant teasing I suffered from childhood playmates, and even some adults, who used my most-hated nickname "Shake-a-Plenty." They thought it was funny, but they had no idea as to how much emotional pain or shame I felt each time I heard those taunts. I couldn't understand why these memories were flooding my mind now, right when I was about to experience a re-dedication of the renewed inner-life that Jesus Christ died to give me.

Finally, I decided to shift my focus and thank God I wasn't born with extreme manifestations of fetal alcohol syndrome.

My attention was quickly drawn to the woman standing behind me. I turned to smile and say good evening, and I noticed she was shaking intensely from head to toe. At first I thought she was experiencing a nervous disorder. She smiled and greeted me. Even her voice was shaking. It rattled. "I'm so nervous, but I don't know why."

Without forethought, I took her hand and said, "It's okay to be nervous, God understands." What? I could not believe I was hearing those words come out of my mouth—not Miss Queen of Trembling Hands and Shaking Knees.

However, as we engaged in light conversation, something happened; I noticed while the woman trembled even more, God drew my attention away from her and made me aware of a "foreign stillness" of my own hands. After forty-seven years of experiencing the feeling and sight of my hands trembling and feeling the agony of inner shame, that night God had "stilled" my hands. So, as I slowly climbed towards the baptismal pool, I could not believe my eyes; I quickly did a double-glance to make sure that those were really my hands.

Suddenly, I realized that my name was being called to step into the baptismal pool. I sat on the bench, and my pastor smiled and asked, "What are you doing here?" He appeared to be puzzled that I was being baptized; after all, I had been a Christian for many years.

I responded, "Tonight, I am surrendering in total submission to God's will and purpose for my life." As I was emerging from the water, God had me take special note, that for those brief moments, the hand tremors were all gone.

I walked out of the water, and one of the greeters said, "Sheila, you are trembling all over."

This time instead of feeling ashamed, I just smiled and walked silently away as I heard God reminding me of the words he had spoken to me so many times before during the most difficult times of my Christian journey, "You are not shaking; you are living in peace in Jesus Christ."

However, a few weeks after that moment, my hands began to tremble more intensely than ever before. Well, I decided that if God had done it once in forty-seven years, then he could do it again. So, I decided to put my faith on trial and walk out my healing in prayer. As I walked on the nature trail, I raised my trembling hands towards heaven just as I had done so many times before, and with a loud voice of expectancy, I declared Psalm 139:13 (KJV). *"For you created my inmost being; you knit me together in my mother's womb. Father, my trembling hands were part of that creation. God I am asking you to either show me its purpose for your glory or stop the tremors."*

As I slowly lowered my trembling hands, first I thanked God for the past moments of tremor-free hands and told Him that if I had to have trembling hands until he called me home, then I would accept it by His grace. Then I decided to take God at His word and prayed Psalm 103:1, 3 (NIV). *"Praise the LORD, my soul; all my inmost being, praise his holy name. Who forgives all your sins and heals all your diseases."*

Today, I feel blessed to say that God has healed me from the hand tremors. I am no longer in bondage to the enemy's attempt to hold me in captivity to shame. I am free in Jesus Christ for all eternity. To God be the glory, I am free of the shame from what others may say or think of me or any other imperfections that remain in me. Today, I can testify that my God is a healer and the lifter of my hands.

The journey to my inner strength of "I'm not shaking, I'm living in peace." is a testimony to the faithfulness of God's promises to strengthen His children to withstand every momentary and light affliction for a more eternal weight of glory. By faith, I now declare, Yes! I am not shaking, I am living in peace.

ABOUT THE AUTHOR

Sheila L. Mills, MPH, CPM is a public health administrator, Christian author, and life-purpose speaker. Sheila's passion is to glorify God by inspiring others to discover and excel in their true kingdom-purposed life as promised in Jeremiah 29:11. Sheila's message for victorious living is to declare: "I am coming out of this! Pray, think, plan, and act like it's going to happen." She currently lives with her husband Bruce and family in North Charleston, South Carolina.

You can learn more about this author at:
http://faithwriters.com/testimonies.php

GOD BELIEVES IN ME?

By Shann Hall-LochmannVanBennekom

Each person experiences several pivotal moments in life that write on the slate of who they are. Just after I turned eighteen, I experienced such a time.

To make sure no one I knew saw me, I glanced over my shoulder before entering the college health center. Once inside, I crouched in a corner and filled out the health questionnaire.

My heart pounded when the nurse called my name. After answering her questions and providing a urine sample, I waited for her to return.

"The test is positive. You're pregnant. What are you going to do?"

The room spun as my fears became a reality. I buried my face in my hands and mumbled, "Cry."

She reached out and patted my shoulder. "Then what?"

Wiping the tears away, I lifted my head. "I guess talk to my mom."

The nurse's eyes widened. "Wow, I've never heard that answer before." She handed me some information, and then sent me on my way.

My head reeled as different thoughts bombarded me. After telling my boyfriend, we agreed we each would talk to our parents alone. Even though it was Mom's birthday, I knew I needed to tell to her then, or I might never muster the courage. I walked into the living room, and my stomach plunged when I saw her sleeping on the couch. Licking my lips, I reached over and shook her. "Mom, wake up; I'm pregnant."

Terrified that I had disappointed my parents, I held my breath.

Mom cried and said, "How could you do this to us?" It took a few days for the news to sink in, but soon they both came to terms with the situation and promised to support me.

Though telling my parents was difficult, a few months later, my world crumbled when my boyfriend dumped me. Overwhelmed by the pregnancy, the break-up, and the difficult decisions that awaited me, I called a friend. "I have proof that there isn't a god. It says in the Bible that God will never give you more than you can handle. Well, this is too much. I can't handle it; therefore, there is no god."

He didn't hesitate before answering. "The only thing that proves is that God has more faith in you than you have in yourself."

That blew me away. I had never considered the fact that God believed in me. The more I thought about it, the stronger I became. My problems didn't disappear overnight, but when complications appeared, I didn't fall apart. Instead, I reminded myself that God believed I could handle this. As it turned out, the so-called-disaster resulted in one of the three best things in my life—my first daughter.

A few years later, I found myself dealing with a different life-altering situation. Sores popped out all over my body. It felt as if someone had sprinkled acid on me. Months later, the doctors diagnosed me with post-herpetic neuralgia from a shingles-like virus. Usually, the virus doesn't travel throughout the body, but I had excruciating lesions all over, from the lining of my brain to the bottom of my feet.

Now, almost twenty-five years later, the longest time the virus has been in remission is three months. Even after the sores heal, the pain stays. There are spots on my body where the gentlest of touch feels like someone is trying to electrocute me. I often wake up screaming, and then worry that I could be scarring my children emotionally.

When they were younger, I would try to stay awake so I could muffle the screams in my pillow, but sleep deprivation just made the cycle worse. The kids would beg me to go to the hospital to get the antiviral and pain medications that would allow me to endure the outbreak.

The doctors initially promised me the pain would go away as quickly as it came, but I've now reconciled that God has other plans. I may not always know how God uses my illness to glorify his name, but I have no doubt that his fingerprints are all over my situation. When I listen and do things on his timetable instead of mine, wonderful things happen, and I am able to witness to people whom I might never have met if not for my illness. Knowing I can comfort others has allowed me to see the purpose in my suffering.

In the early years, it was clear my mom struggled with seeing me suffer. She believed if I had the right attitude, then I would be healed and restored to my former self. She hated when the doctor admitted me to the hospital and prescribed powerful painkillers.

Actually, that was really the only time we argued. It got to the point where I found myself lying to her because she would harass me about needing medication to endure the agony. Though as a mother myself, I understand that helpless feeling when my kids are sick. We are programmed that it's the mother's job to make every-thing better. When Mom couldn't make me better, I believe she felt like she failed me. She constantly would chirp, "Keep your chin up and your eyes on the Lord." Oh, how I grew to resent that line. I needed her to accept the fact that God had other plans for me than healing.

In August 1993, my grandmother passed away in her sleep. The next day, the doctors admitted me to the hospital for a shingles out-break, causing me to miss her funeral. The pain ravished my body, and I vomited whenever I tried to eat or drink. Because I was four months pregnant, the hyperemesis endangered the baby's life as well as my own.

The day after Grandma's funeral, I had an ultrasound and dis-covered I was carrying the second daughter who I desperately had hoped for. I called Mom and squealed with excitement.

"So, I guess it's a girl?" She laughed as I giggled with delight.

It thrilled me to share this news with Mom, but then she gave me the best gift ever. "Honey, I've prayed, and am placing you in God's hands. The doctors know the best way to treat your pain. I promise I won't hassle you about taking the medicine ever again."

Later, I wondered if she had an inkling of what lay ahead. The next day, Mom had three cranial aneurysms rupture. She never spoke to me again. Those final words still echo in my head—a reminder of Mom's unconditional love and God's omnipotence.

I didn't think I could survive losing my best friend, my spiritual mentor, and my mother, but Jesus gave me the strength I needed. Now, twenty years later, my heart still hurts and I miss her so much. There are times when the physical pain overwhelms me, and I beg God to let me die. Even in the midst of the darkest nights, I hear these words whispered in my ear, "Keep your chin up and your eyes on the Lord because Jesus believes in you!"

Throughout these ordeals, I've learned that God's love is everpresent. It is a relief to believe in a powerful God, but what calms me most is the knowledge that a powerful God believes in me.

ABOUT THE AUTHOR

Shann Hall-LochmannVanBennekom and her husband, Christopher, have three kids: Emily, Quinten, and Lydia, and they live in in Dansville, New York, USA. Shann used to be an OB/GYN nurse before her illness forced her to stop working. Her first picture book is due to be released at the end of 2013. Shann enjoys helping other writers by editing and critiquing.

To see more of her work, go to:
http://faithwriters.com/testimonies.php

GOD'S VIEW
IS BETTER THAN OURS

By Sally Stap

*"How long, O Lord, must I call for help? But you do not listen!
'Violence is everywhere!' I cry, but you do not come to save."
(Habakkuk 1:2, NLT)*

I was stunned to be diagnosed at age fifty-one with a brain tumor. With surgery looming a month away, I sought serenity by walking in the woods. I found bravery through prayer, Bible reading, friends, and family. I displayed a great front by demonstrating courage in adversity. I believed it would be tough but admittedly didn't expect any long-term consequences in my life because I was a Christian and felt protected. Following recovery, I planned to step right back into life with a wonderful story to share. But God had other plans.

I reluctantly showed up at the appointed time for brain surgery. I can't say I showed up because I wanted to be a beacon for God. I showed up because the alternative was death. I inhaled, exhaled, and went to sleep for a nine-hour surgery.

When I awoke, my head screamed without ceasing. I had naïvely hoped to retain my hearing, but was deaf in my right ear with a loud ringing in my head. I wasn't expecting to awaken with a half-paralyzed face—but I did, a result that doctors had predicted, and I had ignored. I groaned when I learned that we wouldn't know "if or when any facial movement would return, but it would probably be at least six months..." I didn't have time for that.

My heart sunk a bit further when doctors sewed a titanium

weight into my eyelid to help my eye close. What? That sounded long-term. I was surprised to learn I could no longer write as my hand shook relentlessly when holding a pen. The good news? The brain tumor had been removed. Imagine "Yay" in a very weak voice.

After two months of intense head pain, it was clear I would not be returning to work. Hopeful that with "just a couple more months of healing" I would improve, I pushed. I looked carefully in the mirror each day, hoping for any sign of movement in my face. However, pushing in some circumstances does nothing. I learned the meaning of waiting on God in stillness.

Post-surgery head pain is characterized by periods of almost normal days followed by crushing days or nights filled with demoralizing and immobilizing pain. Single-sided deafness is more than simply reducing two-sided hearing by half. I couldn't tell where sound was coming from, and my brain could no longer filter background noise. In an attempt to turn up the volume when hearing nothing, the brain brings loud ringing into the mix. Months passed. At seven months, my face began to show movement, which then morphed into abnormal movement. I mourned the loss of my smile.

I was disappointed in God. There was no miracle showing God's love. I wasn't adding value to life by not being able to return to work. I went to Florida and walked on the beach. I pouted. I slipped into depression, disability, and faithlessness. After all, how could I praise a God who would allow this to happen?

> *"Oh my God, you alone can rescue me…"*
> *(Psalms 51:14, NLT)*

Slowly, my mind calmed and I accepted the new me. I studied David in an attempt to climb out of a deep depression. If he could recover with the turmoil and sin in his life, maybe I could recover, too. In hindsight, I saw that God had cared for me in the background, as He had explained to Habakkuk. He knew my needs before I knew they would exist. At work, we had established long-term disability policies one year before my diagnosis, providing financial support. I moved from New Jersey to Michigan one year prior to my diagnosis, bringing me closer to family. My youngest daughter was home for a visit when I came home from the doctor with the news, providing emotional support through that first day and night. My other daughter wasn't working, freeing her to be my "research assistant" and my caregiver at the hospital. My parents lived nearby.

"This vision is for a future time. It describes the end, and it will be fulfilled. If it seems slow in coming, wait patiently, for it will surely take place. It will not be delayed."
(Habakkuk 2:3, NLT)

Slowly I grieved and let go of my old self. I still felt pleasure, even while in pain. I learned that laughter is the tone of victory over hurt and pain. Giving thanks to God in everything is not always easy, but it helps us see things more clearly. Praising God allowed me to focus on Him and not myself. Focusing on God brought me peace gradually, over time, as I was finally able to quiet my mind and heart.

Today I can tell you the best time to walk on the beach to find fascinating things is after a storm when the tide goes out. A few years ago I couldn't tell you that because I hadn't lived by the ocean. Who we are and what we know changes daily. What we care about is tweaked or rocked, changing our life perspective continuously. I have learned to manage pain and cram living into low pain moments. When I can't, I focus on God, His love, and His ability to bring peace into my life.

"And give thanks for everything to God the Father in the name of our Lord Jesus Christ." (Ephesians 5:20, NLT)

Like ocean tides, life comes in waves of relationships and life events. Good and bad experiences knock us off our feet and we tumble, breathless, not knowing which way is up. As we figure it out, we rebalance in the sands of life, just in time to feel the next wave. The ocean never stops. Neither does God's love. Regardless of what I've done in my life. Regardless of what comes next. Regardless of the presence or absence of pain.

"O Lord, listen to my prayers; give me the common sense
you promised." (Psalms 119:169, NLT)

We get wrapped up in trying to answer unanswerable questions. Through hindsight and faith, we learn to trust that He has the best answer. We are looking at the problem, and He is looking over it. Yes, I'm disappointed that my head still hurts. I'm frustrated and embarrassed that my face doesn't smile normally. But I know God takes pleasure in my life and each little success as I climb the recovery cliff. I've learned to ask the Holy Spirit for help with my prayers. I ask for guidance on how to pray and am reminded to focus on God. Redirecting my mind to Him brings peace.

"Be still, and know that I am God!" (Psalms 46:10, NLT)

So, I breathe. I accept the facts of my faith. God is. Jesus died for me. All else is noise. He takes pleasure in my life. God is right here, helping me feel peace as I reach up to him, only to find he's already next to me taking weight from life's burdens.

"Yet God has made everything beautiful for its own time.
He has planted eternity in the human heart, but even so,
people cannot see the whole scope of God's work from
beginning to end." (Ecclesiastes 3:11, NLT)

ABOUT THE AUTHOR

Sally lives near family in Kalamazoo, Michigan, USA. After a successful Information Technology career, she shifted to writing in the hope that her experience will bring reassurance and inspiration to others. She is the author of the book Smiling Again: Coming Back to Life and Faith after Brain Surgery.

To read more of her work, go to:
http://faithwriters.com/testimonies.php.

I AM NOT ALONE

By Amber Leggette-Aldrich

As I watched my eight year old son die in my hands, knowing there was absolutely nothing I could do to save him, I was brought into the deepest despair imaginable. I truly wished I was dead myself.

On that day, Christian, an active, healthy boy, was out enjoying a ride on his snowmobile with his father, when he stopped long enough to give me a hug. His father had gone back out to the trail, and in a hurry to catch up, Christian was going too fast to stop at the end of the driveway. As he slid out into the road, he was struck by a truck which then ran over Christian and his machine.

I heard the crash, and my heart stopped for a moment. When I arrived at the scene, all I could see of Christian was his head sticking out from under the rear tire of the truck which was sitting directly on top of his chest. As I dropped down into the snow beside him, I gently lifted his head into my hands and began praying, alternating with cries for help and telling Christian that I loved him. His eyes were partly open, and he was trying to breathe, but the weight of the truck was crushing him.

I watched in horror as his eyes glazed over, and his face turned blue. Then, suddenly, I remembered the verse from Mark 10:27 (AMP); *"Jesus glanced around at them and said, With men [it is] impossible, but not with God; for all things are possible with God."* I had no idea how it could be possible for God to save my son, but, in faith, I continued to pray. I was feeling dizzy at that point, but I remember crying out with all my heart, "I have faith in You and I trust You completely! I'm putting my baby in Your hands because You are mighty and capable. I know in my heart that You will heal him and make him whole again, if not here on earth, then in Heaven!"

It took over twenty minutes for the first rescue vehicle to arrive. In the meantime, Jimmy, Christian's dad, had gone to get his truck with a winch to pull the other truck up off of Christian. As Jimmy and the paramedics began lifting the truck up, they realized that Christian's leg was wrapped around the rear axle. They had to stop and dig under the truck to free his leg before they could pull him out. As soon as they pulled his body out to the road, they began CPR, and continued for over forty minutes. Only by a miracle did they finally get a faint pulse back, and then he was taken to the hospital by helicopter.

Hours later, the head doctor of the pediatric intensive care unit came out and spoke with Jimmy and me. "I'm sorry; there's just too much damage. Christian's hearts and lungs have been crushed. He has severe head trauma, and his liver is lacerated. He has several fractured ribs, and his right leg was nearly torn off, plus it has a compound fracture. There is nothing we can do." She paused and placed her hand on my shoulder. "I'm sorry, but Christian won't make it through the night. You should go and be with him now. Hold him, and love him while you still can."

I remember, as I heard her words, a feeling came over me. It was like a blanket of love, and somehow I *knew* that things would work out. I had no explanation, except that it was God speaking to my heart.

Christian remained in a coma for four days, and there were many up and downs. But through it all, I knew God was right there with us, and I knew He was holding Christian in His arms.

After Christian came out of the coma, he said something to me that changed me forever. "Am I still in Heaven?"

I said, "No son, you're in the hospital."

He became agitated and looked me straight in the eye. "Why did you take me away from Jesus? I didn't want to leave!"

Later, he told me about sitting on Jesus' lap and how beautiful it was. Then he said, "I remember the most beautiful glowing steps,

114

and Jason led me down through the angels and back to the gate."

Jason was my oldest son. He had died the month before Christian was born.

Against all odds, and to the total amazement of all the doctors, Christian was fully recovered, with the exception of his leg. He was released from the hospital just twenty days after his accident. After enduring several surgeries, his leg is now fully healed as well.

The doctors, nurses, paramedics, and even the helicopter pilot have all told me the same thing...while they all did what they were trained to do, in Christian's case, it was not their hands that saved him, but God's.

Christian explained, "We're not alone. God is always right here with us, and He loves us all very much."

My heart has been touched by God in a way that words can never fully explain. Words like thankfulness, trust, faith, hope, and love barely even begin to scratch the surface of what I feel. God took what started out as a horrible tragedy and turned it into a blessing of many miracles, not just for me and my family, but for many others as well. I am truly privileged to be a witness to His great love and power.

There was a time in my life when I had no faith. I didn't even believe in God. I can look back now, however, and see so many times when He was reaching out to me, speaking to my heart. I just wasn't listening, but there was emptiness inside of me, and it was excruciating. When I finally asked Him, God filled the emptiness and healed the hurting.

I can say with all certainty that there is not always a happy ending that *we can see*. Sometimes life just doesn't work out the way we want it to. In the two years since Christian's accident, I've gone through many more trials. Things like financial difficulties, natural disasters, health issues, and most recently, the death of my mother are just a few of the issues that I've had to face. However, there is a promise in the bible that says, *"I can do all things through Christ which strengtheneth me." (Philippians 4:13, KJV)* I've learned that even though I can't always see how things will work out, it doesn't really matter. As long as I allow Christ to give me the strength I need, I know together we can get through the difficult trials that life brings. I know I'm in God's hands, and everything will be alright. No matter what I may have to go through, I feel His presence right here with me, and I trust Him completely. I am not afraid because I know...*I am not alone!*

ABOUT THE AUTHOR

A writer by trade, Amber Leggette-Aldrich's mission in life is to share hope and encouragement in Jesus Christ with everyone she meets. Her speaking engagements have included Kings Church in Wasilla, Alaska, and the 2012 EMS State Conference for Alaska. She lives, works and plays in the mountains of Alaska, where she shares a small cabin with her youngest son.

To read more of Amber's work, go to:
http://faithwriters.com/testimonies.php

MY 9/11

By Ken Ebright

On Tuesday, September 11th, my world changed forever. This 9/11 occurred in 1979, twenty-two years earlier than the infamous 9/11 of 2001. That day I attended my mom's funeral.

About a month earlier, I had come home from playing outside when I found a letter with a key taped to it on the kitchen table. It was from my mom and said she was going to jump off a bridge. I felt confused because I couldn't understand why she would want to do this. I asked my mom about it, and she told me she was mad. Because I was fourteen, I didn't have the maturity to realize she was crying out for help.

The Saturday before Labor Day, as I went into the house, my mom was pulling out of the driveway. Around eleven o'clock that evening, I started to wonder why my mom hadn't returned home yet. The dog was sleeping on the carpet next to the door. I sensed my dad was restless because he was playing solitaire in his basement office. This was not normal for him.

The next day my mom still wasn't home. I remembered the note I had found on the kitchen table a few weeks earlier. I hopped on my bike and went to find her. I found her car at the Bloomington Ferry Bridge. I pedaled furiously back home and told my dad. We both jumped into the car and raced to the bridge. I had never seen my dad drive so crazy in my whole life. He called the police while we were waiting. I remembered him screaming, "Liz, I loved you!" A week later, they found the remains of my mom's body in the Minnesota River.

My mom's life had started to fall apart when her mom died of a heart attack. It was about that time when I realized she was drinking.

She would get into numerous fights with my dad. Late on one hot summer night, our dog barked, and the neighbors started to yell at my mom. Then she started arguing with the people next door. This would play out many other times; sometimes my mom would call the police.

My mom had struggled with learning problems her whole life. Graduating from nursing school was one of her greatest accomplishments. Even though she may have needed to take extra classes, I know my dad had offered to help her with her studies.

I inherited her learning disability. The kids in school knew about it; they teased me and called me stupid.

I have never doubted that there is a God. How can anyone look at creation and say there is no God? I can see his hand in my life. He has always put people in my life to help me at the right time.

I am thankful I attended a Christian school. Because of my learning disabilities, it probably would have been better educationally for me to attend a public school since my school didn't have the resources to help me with my challenges. But it was more important that I be grounded in the faith that would guide me throughout my life. I often wonder how my life would have turned out if I hadn't had the influence of the Christian school.

Ignorance is bliss; I didn't realize how bad my life was as a child. My dad married my stepmom and found a psychiatrist who started the process of helping me deal with my emotional problems. I was able to see that my mom was sick. It's hard for to me to admit, but my stepmom was a blessing. Had she not come into my life, I don't know where I would be. I might have ended up in jail or worse.

He takes care of his people like a shepherd. He gathers them like lambs in his arms. (Isaiah 40:11a NCV)

When I look back over my life, I believe Jesus carried me through my childhood. I didn't fully comprehend that I could ask him for help. Several years after my mom's death, a former classmate of mine was struck by a car. At the wake, her mom told me she had prayed for me. I may never know on this side of Heaven how many people prayed for me and my family.

Now that I've grown in my faith and have seen how God has carried me close to him, how could I doubt him? When I moved to Illinois, the Lord cared enough about me that he chastened my life. Because I grew up in a broken home, I wasn't living like a child of the King. I thank the Lord that I am not the same person I was ten years ago.

In spite of my mistakes, the Lord has put people in my life to help me. My former pastor helped me get my current job. Now, I have employers who care about me personally and want to do everything they can to help me financially. A man in my Bible study fixes my car for way less than what a regular mechanic would charge. Every night that I have a warm bed to sleep in, I praise the Lord. I don't deserve what I have, but God has provided.

When the sky gets dark, and the wind starts to blow, I just need to trust in the Lord.

ABOUT THE AUTHOR

Ken Ebright lives in the United States in Belleville, Illinois. He considers himself a native Minnesotan. Ken plays a keyboard instrument and sings in a men's choir.

To read more about Ken, go to:
http://faithwriters.com/testimonies.php

MY JERICHO WALL

By Amy Michelle Wiley

"You need to think about pursuing a different career." My professor shifted in her office chair. "You have retaken classes, but show no improvement."

No improvement. The words echoed in my head the rest of the day. They rang as a denial against all the hours and pain I had poured into training to become a sign language interpreter. I clung to the one thing I knew. God had called me to this. How it would be accomplished, I did not know.

A few hours later, I sat across from James, my Deaf tutor and mentor. We conversed easily in American Sign Language (ASL)—when it was just chatting, and then, came time to get to work. He laid out five children's flash cards with bright, simple pictures. After giving me a few seconds to look at them, he covered them up. "What were they?"

"A flower..." My fingers spread into a bloom. "And..." I searched my memory bank. The pictures had been in front of me seconds ago. Easy-peasy.

James waited.

A kindergartener task and I had nothing.

He moved on to the next exercise and fingerspelled a word slowly. I'd known the ASL alphabet fluently for ten years; yet the shapes slipped from my mind as fast as his hand moved to the next letter.

I finally grasped a fragment of a word and scribbled: *Ball*

He crossed it out and wrote *lab* underneath.

I couldn't hold in the doubts and pain. Tears burned behind my eyes as my hands flew. "The teachers in the program have made it clear they don't think I can make it. None of them believe in me." I met his gaze. "Can I do this? Do you think I can really overcome my learning disabilities to become a good interpreter?"

The weight of my question hung between us. He had already spent hours with me, working on basic visual memory skills as well as the more complicated language skills all the students were learning. He was a Certified Deaf Interpreter and fluent in several languages. I trusted him to know the answer. Even more so, I trusted him to be honest.

"Yes, I think you can."

I cried harder.

"You'll have to work hard, but I do see improvement. You love the language and the culture. When you get past the struggles, you enjoy interpreting. You can do this."

That was all it took. God and James had my back.

I returned to classes, day after day. My teachers shrugged. What was it to them if I wanted to bang my head against a wall? But I knew a secret they didn't. I had a God who specialized in bringing walls down. And sometimes he required what appeared to be foolish action on our part before those cracks started appearing.

One of my classmates pulled me aside. "I've been struggling with the pace of the program and have thought of dropping out, but you inspired me to keep trying."

As my signing gradually grew stronger, my body grew weaker. Health issues I'd dealt with since high school grew significantly worse under the stress of college.

One day I sat waiting for group tutoring time, slumped against the bright yellow plastic of a classroom chair, pain wracking my body. I sucked in a breath, shaking so badly my teeth chattered, and I could hardly make my signing understood.

James caught my eye from across the room and motioned to me.

I stood up, only to have my knees buckle. I lurched forward and grabbed the wobbly side tray of a chair. Halfway across the room, my vision blacked out and the room swirled. Somehow, I caught myself before hitting the floor.

Concern lined James' face, his eyebrows creasing. "I think you should go home."

I gave a wry smile. "You want me to drive the hour home in this condition? Besides, I'd just go home and huddle in a miserable ball. I might as well huddle in a miserable ball in the corner of the classroom and hope I can retain a little of the lectures."

With pure stubbornness, I pushed through the bone-numbing fatigue, pain, memory loss, and a host of other symptoms. Many days I cried through a whole class, but I was there, in the class.

When I would finally collapse at home, Mom cooked me dinners and my sister would quiz me on Deaf culture keywords and linguistic definitions. On the weekends and my off days, I slept. Attending church seemed out of the question most weeks.

Fear nipped at me as the doctors ran tests and shrugged their shoulders. Surely God wouldn't bring me this far just to let me die of cancer or something before I could even graduate.

Soon I had to wear a heart monitor to class, interrupting lectures with its high-pitched beep whenever my heart would start racing or skipping beats. One year, I spent almost nine months clumping around in a medical boot because a wound on my toe would not heal.

Finally I got diagnosed with Fibromyalgia. (Years later a specialist realized I was misdiagnosed and figured out I actually have a genetic disorder instead.) I began the process of accepting, that short of a miracle, I would be facing these symptoms for the rest of my life. God had made it clear he was doing a miracle in my life, but just as clearly it wouldn't be a "*poof* and everything is fixed" one. He was allowing a difficult road, and asking me to make the trek around my own Jericho wall, day after day.

And so I walked on. I again dropped classes and lightened my load; this time it wasn't from inadequacy in skills, but because of my health.

God brought two Christian classmates into my life, Holly and Breezy. The three of us met every week, crowding into a tiny practice room, grabbing a few minutes here and there between classes. We poured out our struggles and discouragement to God about the incredibly challenging content, difficult teachers, and demanding schedule. All around us, other students dropped out.

One day, Breezy found me crying in the corner. I pointed to note on a transcription of one of my interpretations. It had only two words etched in bright red.

Great job!

This time, it was tears of joy.

"You know what's awesome?" Breezy touched the words of encouragement. "It's so clear your accomplishments are only from God. Everyone can see your weak body and know you can't do it. The whole world can see it is God's strength in you."

My journey around my Jericho wall took me six years just to get my associate's degree. In June of 2010, I stood on the stage of an auditorium, and I heard my name ring out. My smile trembled with excitement as the dean shook my hand and handed me my diploma. In a back room, my backpack already held paperwork for a part-time interpreting job.

Over the sound of the audience's applause and my family and friends' cheers, I heard another sound, almost like a trumpet call, and felt a slight tremor under my feet. It was a rumble; the last stone falling from a crumpled wall.

ABOUT THE AUTHOR

Amy Michelle Wiley's love for words and people has led to her work as a freelance author, editor, and as a sign language interpreter. She has a passion for helping new writers get published, and has had over seventy of her own short stories and articles published, as well as publishers interested in her two in-progress novels. Though her work is limited by her disabling health, she is learning to live life fully and joyfully.

Read more from Amy: http://faithwriters.com/testimonies.php

MY LIFEBOAT

By K.D. Manes

Icy hands grasp my ankles, pulling me further into the rancid, slimy pit. "Help!" I cry, weak and confused.

Depression is an invisible, life-sucking phantom. I never thought I would become its prey. However, I found myself fighting this mysterious gloom during my college years.

In high school, I strived for success in academics, sports, and leadership. I enjoyed my friends and cherished my relationship with Christ. However, the combination of late study college nights, doughnut splurging, school transitioning, and high expectations contributed to my hypoglycemia (low blood sugar). This soon spiraled into clinical depression. My thoughts became muddled whenever my blood sugar levels plunged. So diving into sweets helped me focus and feel better, temporarily anyway, before my blood sugar level dipped again.

Looking back, I realize I would have been the perfect candidate for a depression commercial: a slumped girl, hands covering a despairing face while the commentator advocates the need for proper medication. Neither my family nor I knew anything about hypoglycemia, let alone clinical depression and/or treatment options, since it wasn't publicized much in the late eighties.

Long study hours proved futile as both my academic and athletic performance wavered. My interests in sports and outdoor activities waned as anxiety, body aches, and sleepless nights increased. My strong will gradually ebbed into emotional numbness and exhaustion.

The more I fought to stay afloat in daily living, the deeper I sank into despair. Increasing sadness and failure weighed heavily on me.

Who are you? I asked the reflection glaring back at me in the mirror one day. *And where is your God?* The unknown variables of "what" and "why" fueled my anger and guilt.

There were times I wanted to talk to someone about my struggles, but on the surface I appeared healthy. Who would believe I felt broken inside? *If I can't understand what is happening,* I reasoned, *how can anyone else?* As a Christian, I knew joy should be present in my life. *Why can't I get out of this funk?* I often asked myself.

I felt trapped inside a dark, slippery hole. My determination—which had proved useful for past challenges—wasn't enough to bolster me to the surface. Weary of forcing myself through daily motions and masking the pain, I found myself socially retreating more often. This is when the enemy pressed in the most, *"Why keep on like this? ... You can end it ... then you will rest."*

Through my storm, however, God faithfully sprinkled caring people in my path who encouraged me with kind words, or availed themselves as someone to talk with. The Holy Spirit urged me to cry out to God. My test boiled down to trust. Would I cling to my Savior—whom I'd known since a child—believing He had good plans in store for me? Or would I continue to question and give up, discounting His love and ability to heal, change my circumstances, and/or pull me through this dark time?

I knew suicide would be wrong. So, broken and bruised, I dug into the Bible and cried out to Him. That is when the Holy Spirit most often comforted me. He showed me great promises such as Psalm 34:17-19 (NIV), *"The righteous cry out, and the Lord hears them; He delivers them from all their troubles. The Lord is close to the brokenhearted and saves those who are crushed in spirit. A righteous [woman] may have many troubles, but the Lord delivers [her] from them all."*

These were bittersweet times. Although everything dear to me seemed to blow away like chaff in the wind, what I eventually gained far outweighed my conceived loss. The Lord reminded me in 2 Corinthians 4:17 (NLT), *"...our present troubles are small and won't last very long. Yet they produce for us a glory that vastly out-*

weighs them and will last forever!"

Learning to be still and waiting on God wasn't easy. When I did this, however, God's promise in Isaiah 40:28-31 held its weight: when I placed my hope in Him, He infused my inner being with His strength and peace.

I found that the more I read the Bible, the more I longed for His Word. I related to the Psalmist who penned chapter 119:103 (NKJV), *"How sweet are your words to my taste, sweeter than honey to my mouth!"*

Likewise, the more I conversed with my Lord, the more I longed to sit at His feet and absorb His healing, comforting presence. He was—and is—the great *I Am*, who daily bears burdens (Psalm 68:19). He taught me: True success stems from obeying Him. Likewise, failure results from disbelief and disobedience, even when circumstances appear otherwise.

The Lord assured me, my times are in His hands: all the days ordained for me were written in [His] book before one of them came to be (Psalm 31:15; Psalm 139:16); His thoughts toward me outnumber the grains of sand (Psalm 139:17-18); and He delights in me (Psalm 22:8; 147:11).

When I was at my very lowest, His presence became palpable, like a warm healing blanket wrapped around me. Jesus—who experienced the greatest suffering—was with me after all. And He lifted, comforted, and sustained me. Although I had to wait awhile before restoration, I knew His peace. His gentle, loving presence was enough.

In reflection, I don't think I could relate to Paul's declaration about Jesus in Philippians 3:8—*Nothing* compares to His surpassing greatness—had I not needed to cry out to Him in complete dependence. I am grateful I can now confidently share: if the only thing I acquire in this life is a relationship with God through Jesus Christ, I have gained the most valuable treasure of all, both for now and for eternity. I wouldn't trade that for anything.

My "crushed and drooping" days of depression cycled throughout my college years. But God carried me through daily challenges.

After a year of struggling with hypoglycemia, I found some relief from altering my diet. A couple years after that, God granted my doctor wisdom in diagnosing clinical depression. Physical relief came after taking prescribed medication for a couple of months. Slowly and steadily, I found my health, energy, and former interests returning.

Yes, Satan meant me harm, but God used that adversity to grow me in the following areas: 1) Christ-like character; 2) a greater capacity to love and worship God because He preserved my life; 3) more empathy and compassion toward hurting people; 4) greater trust and dependence in Him; and 5) increased security and knowledge of my identity in Jesus Christ.

Thankfully, I haven't struggled again with hypoglycemia or depression. And God enabled me to graduate with an Elementary and Special Education teaching degree, which I have since used and enjoyed. He has also blessed me with a wonderful husband and three fun-loving kids.

Praise God! *For He lifted me out of the slimy pit, out of the mud and mire; He set my feet on a rock and gave me a firm place to stand."* Psalm 40:2 (NIV)

ABOUT THE AUTHOR

K.D. Manes makes her home on the Palouse in eastern Washington, with her husband and three kids. She enjoys outdoor activities with her family, writing children's stories, and outdoor photography.

Her blog and sample articles can be found at the following link:
http://faithwriters.com/testimonies.php

My Name Is On His Hand

By Allison Reed

Without ever giving it any thought, I always knew I would never leave my husband ... but wait ... that was me who just spent five months in a distant city, refusing to come home.

Without even a trace of endurance remaining, I just knew I would never go back ... but wait ... that was me who finally confronted my rebellion, resolving to come home.

The following weeks held challenges, conflicts, and heartaches. My fractured family had not survived the storm. Now, all I could do was sit on my couch with my Bible in my lap and cry out to God. "I know I am of little consequence, but I am your child, God! I need to know you have not forgotten me!"

In the quietness of the room, sunbeams streamed in through the picture window, enveloping me in a special warmth. God's presence embraced me, suffusing me with peace and comfort. The strength gained on that unforgettable, blessed afternoon fortified me for whatever lay ahead. That day, Deuteronomy 33:27 became real for me: *"The eternal God is thy refuge and underneath are the everlasting arms...."*

How I arrived at this place in my life is a tragically familiar story. Through ten years of struggling in a marriage that had never thrived, a seed of unhappiness had taken root. On the surface, I tried to keep a positive attitude; but on this day, it was of no benefit. Thirty years later, the memory is still vivid.

An illicit Father's Day card I was never meant to see conveyed a heart-rending message of rejection, betrayal, and shame. Added words of endearment intensified the shock. For hours, waves of convulsive tremors penetrated to my core. On subsiding, they gave way to pronounced trembling over my entire body as if I were wandering in the Arctic during the fiercest of blizzards. Speaking was impossible for my jaw would not relax enough to form words.

The acrid, bitter taste of adultery has flavored every moment of my life since then.

Though my long-held sense of inadequacy was now established as fact, I wanted my marriage to survive, and I trusted that God would intervene. Though the sacred commitment made at the wedding altar was violated, I chose to believe my husband's assurance that the affair was over, but soon learned that insincere promises don't last long.

The encore to adultery turned out to be unending deception, a ruthless gambling addiction, and disastrous financial decisions.

The binding of my Bible gave out as I continually turned to God's Word for wisdom and direction. Memorizing scripture and listening to gospel music sustained me through the years. I continued to plead with God to make things right, but my relationship and the family's circumstances continued to worsen. In spite of a more than adequate household income, my children were growing up in seeming poverty. That little seed of unhappiness, by then, had grown into a sprawling, invasive vine of depression, feeding on the soil of despondency. Misery shrouded my spirit.

After enduring a second foreclosure, the little hope I still held was obliterated by increasingly irresponsible spending and escalating gambling. Without ever entertaining the thought, I finally knew I would leave, and I did.

Five months later, I conceded that leaving had been the wrong answer. Returning was not easy; staying was even harder.

Then came the worst blow of all. The revelation of ongoing incest tore my heart out, crushed, and pulverized it. All hope for reconciliation vanished, and when divorce happened, I did not resist. The struggle was over, just like that.

Except it wasn't. Marriage right out of high school and thirty years as a stay-at-home mom had left me unprepared to support myself. My future promised homelessness and destitution since I had no place to live and no family to turn to for help. What I did have was a God who had not forgotten me and a church that cared. Because of God's grace, I had the peace that passes understanding. Because of God's people, every need was met. My Jehovah Jireh provided. My smile and joy returned, decimating the embedded tendrils of despair.

Going to college seemed like the logical thing to do, but daunting obstacles confronted me. Aside from my age and the expense, computer and math classes would be an unavoidable torment. Once again, my faithful God enabled. Scholarships, tutors, and three years later, I graduated magna cum laude.

Before a year had passed, I realized that my education had not given me the skills to succeed in my chosen field. I had to settle for clerical work at a meager wage and little else.

Six long years later, I was finally able to move to a different company that offered better money and benefits. I was elated. Ninety long days later, I was convinced of my incompetence and unemployed. I was also devastated.

For weeks, I frantically searched for work, but with the country entrenched in recession, my applications only gathered dust. Eventually, I gave up my apartment and moved to another state to live with my son, but obtaining a job continued to elude me. Even after some promising interviews, even after going through a five month long qualification process, I was never the chosen candidate.

Confusion and discouragement battered me. The rejection and hopelessness of unemployment burrowed relentlessly, unearthing that noxious, persistent, depression vine. With a vengeance it reemerged, spewing vile accusations: *Your pathetic attempts will never amount to anything!* and *Your life is a monument to failure.* The insults kept coming, alternating with: *You are of no value to anyone!* and *You are nothing but a burden.* An ever-deepening vortex beckoned, compelling me to surrender to its relentless draw.

How easy it would have been to surrender, if not for a lifeline of hope that offered a better option. God's Word had the answers I needed. Scripture verses, memorized years earlier, reminded me to think on these things: whatsoever things are true, honest, just, pure, lovely, of good report, things of virtue, and things of praise.* Instead of immersing myself in negative thoughts, I recalled the many times God had seen me through. I brought out my old cassette tapes and CD's and listened to uplifting Christian music. The glorious Sonshine penetrated that deadly, creeping vine and withered it away to nothingness.

Life goes on. I did eventually find employment, a position in which I truly made a difference in the life of one family faced with the heartache of Alzheimer's. My feelings of inadequacy and incompetence are quashed when I think of the outflow of gratitude they expressed as I said goodbye for the final time. I'm back in my home state now, and once again I am unemployed. Once again, I am waiting for God to move. I know He will, in His time. He has already provided for me in amazing ways, and He has infused me with peace about my circumstances. Isaiah 49:16a reminds me, *"Behold, I have engraved you upon the palms of my hands..."* With my eyes fixed on Him, I rejoice that He is a God who cares and will never forsake me.

~~~~~~~~~~~~~~~~~~~~~~~~~~~~~~~~~~~~

Isn't it just like God to provide a new job on the very day I write about His faithfulness? I start next week.

*Paraphrased from Philippians 4:8

ABOUT THE AUTHOR

Allison Reed lives in the United States, and continues to seek the special place where God can bless her and she can be a blessing. Challenges have confronted her in every phase of life, but God has also filled her life with unending blessings that help buffer the pain. Writing, art, friends, family, and, with every breath, Allison's faith in God have all strengthened her for the tasks set before her.

Read more: http://faithwriters.com/testimonies.php

NEVER GIVE UP...
ALWAYS LET GO

By Phyllis Stokes

So many machines crowded the tiny ICU room; there was barely space for anything else—not even a chair for sitting. I had been standing by or walking around Michael's bed for three days, praying non-stop. Michael, my only child, had been airlifted to Syracuse University Hospital after firemen found him unresponsive from smoke inhalation and carbon monoxide poisoning. A fire had started in his apartment while he slept during the night. The smell of smoke, still permeating his body, infused the hospital room.

Fatigued to the point of collapse, I prepared to meet with a team of doctors for another conference. I just hoped they would make it quick. Apparently, they didn't want to waste any time either. The first doctor got right to the point. "Your son's body has already begun to shut down." The words floated around in my head not making a connection. "The best thing you can do now is to let him go."

A second doctor opened the folder in front of him and pulled out a form. "Ms. Stokes, this is a DNR form. Your son has coded several times, and every effort to resuscitate him adds more stress to his body. If he codes again, we strongly recommend not resuscitating him." He paused and softened his voice. "I'm sorry, but with all that has happened, his brain is mush."

I took a deep breath, trying to stop the room from spinning. *This conversation has to be a mistake.*

I remembered the last conversation I had with Michael. Since he moved away to New York after high school, we had not been together much. "We have lots to talk about Momma," he told me over the phone. Michael, being the only child, and I, the only parent, confided in each other a lot. He was an easy child to raise, a pretty good student, most times obedient, always of good manner. Even at the age of ten, he took his role as "man of the house" seriously.

Once while playing in front of the house with a group of kids, some of the kids called me Barney as I passed by in my purple jumpsuit. Michael decided he would take on the whole bunch of them and defend my honor. Outnumbered, he stormed into the house looking for an equalizer. I stopped him just as he was heading out the door with a broom handle. We laughed about it later that night. In later years, as life happened, we drifted apart. But lately, Michael had been thinking it was time for a change.

"I want to come see you soon," he continued.

"How 'bout Thanksgiving?"

"Yeah...okay. Thanksgiving. I love you Momma."

"I love you too, Son."

We never made it to Thanksgiving. Instead, on a hot day in August, I sat in a cold, sterile room, numb; a team of doctors trying to convince me my son's life was over. Their words ricocheted from the invisible shield I had placed over my heart. Still, I battled the raging war of my own thoughts. *Oh, God! They say that if he wakes up, he will be a vegetable at best. Am I holding on to something that You have said is over? Michael looks so tortured. His big brown eyes wide open; lifelessly staring into nothing. Is he begging me to let him go? Am I just prolonging his suffering?*

I stretched out my hand to reach for the form. "Where do I sign?" At the same time, I silently pleaded with God for Michael's life.

"Do you have any questions?"

As I walked toward the door, I shook my head and kept walking until I reached Michael's room. I stood there watching his chest rise violently, vibrating the entire bed as the oscillator pumped 300 beats per minutes into his lungs. A picture of Michael going into distress and no one trying to resuscitate him flashed in my mind. Nausea sank to the bottom of my stomach. I had to get out of the room fast. I rushed out, heading for the hospital chapel. Barely crossing the threshold, I sprawled my body across the floor.

Stretched beyond my physical, mental, and emotional capacity I screamed, "God!!! I don't know what to do!" I pressed my face deeper into my hands. "Please God… if Michael's heart stops, my heart will stop." In that moment, I knew I had to risk complete honesty. "God if You don't answer this prayer; I honestly don't know how I can ever pray another prayer."

Suddenly, my mind sobered. "God, You are bigger than what I feel. You are my God, Michael belongs to You. If You give me the grace, I will pray and I will serve You for the rest of my life…**with or without Michael.** But if his life is over, pleeease don't let him suffer like this. Just take him now!"

Those four words ruptured the depths of my being, rotating everything inside. I let out a deep, agonized wail. People outside the chapel rushed in to see what was going on. Assuring them I was okay, I sat down until they left. In the quietness, I remembered something I always told Michael when things got tough. "Son, never give up—no matter what." I headed back to ICU to look for one of the doctors.

"Doctor, I want to disregard the DNR I just signed. I understand that there is nothing more you can do, but I can't just give up. Just continue doing everything medically possible. His life is in God's hands." After all our previous conversations, I expected resistance. Instead, the doctor assured me they would continue, despite his belief Michael would not make it.

I went back to Michael's room and walked as close to the bed as I could. I needed to know Michael was ready for whatever happened—that he had made peace with God. "Son, I want to talk to you." I didn't know if he could hear me, but I hoped he did. "The doctors don't know what to do anymore, but I know that God can do ANYTHING. I have released you completely to God for His will to be done. As much as I love you, He loves you more." His comatose, swollen body just laid there—tubes in his mouth, nose and throat, a host of IV needles in both arms, his limbs blistered and turning charcoal black from lack of circulation.

"I need to know for myself that you have made peace with God. Would you pray with me? Just repeat the words in your heart." Moving in a little closer to his ear, I prayed out loud giving him time to repeat each sentence. "Lord, I confess my sin and ask You to forgive me. Jesus died for me and through His shed blood; I can be cleansed, forgiven and saved. I accept Jesus as my Lord and Savior. Thank You for saving me." *It's up to You, Lord. I trust you.*

That night I curled up in a chair outside Michael's room and went to sleep for the first time in three days. In the morning, Michael was still alive—all vital signs stable.

ABOUT THE AUTHOR

An emerging writer, Phyllis Stokes' desire is to effectively give to multitudes, what she has freely received, and still receives daily—the gospel message of hope to the hopeless, healing to the bruised, and deliverance to the bound. A happily-single parent of one adult son, she currently resides in the US.

To read more about her, go to:
http://faithwriters.com/testimonies.php

THE BLESSING

By Phee Paradise

The fourth day my son was in a coma was Mother's Day. A friend had found Neal too weak to get out of bed after he missed a college final. At the emergency room they diagnosed a stroke caused by leukemia. Family joined us in the waiting room while we prayed and waited and prayed some more. Pleas for healing rose up from all over the world. His school posted hourly updates for the students. His friends brought pictures of him and waited with us. Strangers donated blood and plasma. The elders of our church anointed him with oil and prayed for healing.

As Neal's body sank into septic shock, the doctors said there was no more hope and the nurses cried with us. I read God's promises in the Bible and gave him up to my Father who had watched His Son die. I hated what was happening to my son, but through my tears I could say, "It is well with my soul." Even then, I knew God's blessing.

The blessing was the support of God's people. The blessing was the comfort that came in answer to their prayers. The blessing was the peace that passes understanding.

The next day my son opened his eyes.

With a smile, the neurologist told us, "He's in there."

Gradually he responded to our touch and voices. He squeezed my hand and smiled. He moved and talked and laughed. He learned to walk and feed himself and think again.

Six weeks later, we brought him home and helped him adjust to a new life with some disabilities. We played Scrabble and he learned to make longer words. He taught himself to type and tie his shoes one-handed. Eventually he took a college class and was able to complete it with no evidence of brain damage. We relished his presence while we learned about leukemia and waited for a bone marrow transplant.

The blessing was that on Mother's Day, my son didn't die. The blessing was that he opened his eyes and looked at me. The blessing was that God gave me His Son and also gave me back mine.

Trips to the cancer clinic allowed the doctors to monitor the leukemia. Within four months, three bone marrow donors had been found. Neal entered the hospital for a transplant on the first anniversary of the destruction of the Twin Towers. It was a day of mourning and of hope. I clung to the hope, knowing God had already done so much.

I went to the hospital from work every day. My husband and daughter joined us whenever they could. We played games wearing latex gloves, with alcohol wipes nearby in case we dropped one of the pieces on the floor. Even with the gloves, we weren't allowed to touch him. We also wore masks to prevent our germy breath from reaching him.

The blessing was that I could spend a couple of hours each day playing Sorry or Pitch or Cribbage with my son. The blessing was that he was able to play games. The blessing was that God had given us time.

Neal said his days dragged and he watched for me, tired of movies and books. In his private room he said he was lonely, but he wasn't alone. Nurses came and went, changing his IV drips and bringing him chemotherapy pills that were so toxic he had to wear gloves to put them in his mouth. A nurse hung a calendar on the wall, where she wrote his blood counts every day. We watched them plummet until he had no white cells and almost no red cells or platelets. His immune system had been destroyed.

One day we didn't play games. That day we all three came to the hospital and waited for the donor's bone marrow. The hospital room felt crowded when the doctor and nurse came in to give him the life-giving blood. He slept, but we watched the slow drip, praying there wouldn't be a reaction. The doctor let me hold his hand.

The blessing was that he had the best medical care in the country. The blessing was that someone had willingly shared her healthy bone marrow with him. The blessing was that God was present while we scarcely dared breathe.

When I arrived the next day, he pulled on his gloves, ready for a game of Cribbage. The calendar still showed no white cells, but he said he felt fine. We played every day, while the numbers hovered just above zero. Infection was a constant threat, and they brought his food on specially wrapped trays to avoid bacteria. But he didn't eat much because his mouth hurt. He didn't talk either, but he could still beat me, with a barely visible smile.

One day he was sleeping when I arrived. There were some new gadgets by his bed, a button to push for pain relief and a big plastic tube to spit blood. The cells in his mouth had broken down and he had stopped eating. I sat by his bed and prayed for healing.

Gradually the numbers on the calendar rose, one tenth at a time. Joy! The new bone marrow was making blood cells. His mouth started to heal and we took out the game boards again. After six weeks he began to eat and they let us bring him home. I scrubbed my house of germs, but I could finally hug him. We still played games, but now we didn't wear gloves.

The blessing is that he is in complete remission. The blessing is that it has been more than ten years—years of hugs and games and joy. The blessing is that God is good.

ABOUT THE AUTHOR

Phee Paradise is a freelance writer with diverse writing experiences. Her work includes book reviews, newspaper articles and short stories, and devotionals for her blog, DelightedMeditations.blogspot.com. She resides in South Carolina where she teaches public speaking and volunteers at her church.

You can see some of her work at:
http://faithwriters.com/testimonies.php.

THE HEALING HAND
OF PERFECT GRACE

By Melissa Doerksen

I Was 19

One wintery Monday morning, a friend had seen my sister's car on Highway 1. My mother had been in the car, too, and there was a horrendous car wreck. Not wanting to believe the news, my friend and her boyfriend picked me up at work, and we started in that direction. Nothing could have prepared me as we drew near to the scene ahead. A crushed hunk of metal wrapped around a light pole. *The news report must be wrong.* This certainly didn't resemble my sister's car. A lone police officer was stopping traffic and directed us to pull over to the shoulder. All I could do was stare in horror and disbelief.

"Miss, your mother is deceased, did you know that?" asked the officer.

My vision blurred, my mind raced and went blank at the same time. My heart dropped to my feet, and for all I cared at that moment, it could have dropped right through the floorboards of that old truck onto the icy highway. My world shattered. I couldn't grasp those harsh words, no matter how many times they resounded through my mind.

My mother had been an icon of great faith, prayer, patience, and unconditional love for all, especially for her children. She was more than my mother! She was my best friend, confidante, prayer warrior, and my source of strength, wisdom, and love. People like her were beneficial for the world. How could it have been God's plan to take her away from us, without so much as a chance to say good-

140

bye? **God held me tight.**

Seated in the dimly lit funeral home on Wednesday evening, reality blended into a hazy fog for me, and I heard the faint hymns and smelled the mixed fragrance of many floral arrangements. Faces of strangers passed before me. Why were so many people here to view my mother's precious, but lifeless body? Was nothing sacred?

I barely heard a word. My sole focus was on the open velvety casket illuminated at the front of the room. How could this be happening? I must have asked that question a hundred times. Had my sister been driving too fast on the ice?

A comforting voice and smile brought me back from my wayward thoughts. Perhaps everyone was here to comfort; I really wasn't sure.

Pastor Bartel seated himself before me and sincerely asked, "How is your walk with the Lord? This would be a very good time to ensure your salvation."

I knew he spoke the truth. I had not veered off the straight-and-narrow very far. I had made a commitment as an eight-year-old and then decided as a young teenager to be baptized. I really wanted to be sure I would see my Savior and my mother again.

Pastor Bartel and I bowed our heads, and I invited the Lord in and asked forgiveness. A peaceful warmth filled my heart and soul. **God saved me.**

***

I Was 27

The warm wind whisked through the cemetery that autumn afternoon. I gazed down at the tiny white casket, longingly and confused through tear-filled eyes. The words of *Amazing Grace* floated in the distance, yet hollowly were coming from my own mouth as well. Why would my baby boy be allowed to live for only one day? Was that really God's plan for him? For me?

So much confusion melded my thoughts, and I thought back to

the miscarriage of twins just a couple short years earlier.

"God always knows what He is doing," everybody said. Brief comfort and well wishes brought that certain recognizable warmth on the inside. I imagined my mother caring for her three grandchildren, who had already joined her in Heaven. Although brokenhearted, at that thought I felt the mending begin and knew the four of them could frolic about in safety that I could never provide. **God was there and gave me peace.**

***

I Was 30

The dreaded midnight hour arrived, bringing the all-too-often rude awakening with it. Would there ever be respect and maturity in this marriage?

Stripped of clothing and dignity and backed into the corner, I slid down my bedroom wall into a crumpled, cowering heap on the floor. The sheer rejection I had become so familiar with intensified with each blow to the top of my head.

Please God, don't let my babies wake up and see their daddy pummeling Mommy! **God was listening.**

I slowly began to fall into a very restless sleep on the sofa, amazed that I had been sleeping peacefully only two hours earlier. Tears streamed down my cheeks, and thoughts raced through my mind, lingering briefly on each word and action leading up to this moment. Was it not my right to ask my husband where he had been for the last few days? Would these drunken rages and bouts of violence never end? What about all the affairs he was having? This could not possibly be the marriage God had intended for me. Yet this is why I stayed—to honor God and my marriage. God walked with me.

***

I Was 32

My world turned upside down. I knew I had to leave the violence, infidelity, and the insanity that had become a way of life. Friends, co-workers, and townspeople all seemed to say either aloud or silently, "Well, now look at you. What will you do as a divorced mother of three young children? Are you setting a good example for them? Perhaps you deserved being hit all the time? Maybe you weren't a good wife? Perhaps you are not beautiful enough? To top it all off, you call yourself a Christian. Wow, Christians don't ever get divorced, you know." The enemy's relentless questions sneered and judged me continuously. I felt every eye upon me at the grocery store, in the workplace, and especially at church. **God strengthened me and poured out His Mercy upon me.**

***

I Was 36

Could I really start over? The month of May held happy, new beginnings and brought a fresh excitement. My children accompanied me down the grand staircase at Pinewood Lodge with our guests looking on. We joined Mike, who waited at the beautiful fireplace. Before God and our family and friends, we exchanged marital vows.

My new husband placed the shining wedding band on my left hand. I looked into his beautiful brown eyes and felt God's love and grace pour down on me. I was blessed beyond comprehension as Mike knelt and vowed to love my (our) three children. The spring clouds burst forth into a dazzling sun shower.

"You may kiss your bride," Pastor Neufeld said.

We leaned in until our lips touched. It was an amazing kiss and sealed our freshly made vows, promoting a second chance at a wholesome and moral life. We both desired to make God the head of our household, and wisdom and discernment prevailed. **God redeemed me and began healing me.**

Praise the Lord in all things!

ABOUT THE AUTHOR

Melissa Doerksen writes from the 'Great White North,' also known as Manitoba, Canada. She lives with her husband and three children. Enjoying the great outdoors, especially at the lake, is where she feels closer to God than ever. Continuing to count her blessings each day, she includes her love of writing amongst them. She desires to write for Him always and to inspire others to meet and know Him through her words.

You can learn more about this author at:
http://faithwriters.com/testimonies.php.

THE ARGUMENT

By Laura Hawbaker

It was Christmas Eve, and I was arguing with God.

My twenty-seven year old nephew, Ethan, was dying of Ewing Sarcoma, bone cancer with a notoriously low survival rate. *This absolutely makes no sense,* I quite freely told God. It wasn't death itself that I struggled with, just untimely death.

I gave God a list of people who would gladly die. *God, what about Floyd? He's old and tired and in pain. He is longing for Heaven, and how about Addie? She's so old she thinks you have forgotten her, God.* These old saints had fought a good fight, and were ready to finish the race. It made perfect sense to call them home to their reward! A visit to the nursing home gave me a whole new list of people who should die instead of Ethan. As I walked by a lady picking at a pillow and muttering nonsensical words, I told God what I thought. *God, why don't you take her? She doesn't even know her family. Why is this old lady allowed to live day after day and yet you strike a happily-married man and a father of two with cancer?"*

My sister, Ethan's mother, experiencing the agony of seeing her son become weak and ill, had a great idea. She blogged, "If I were God, I would save Ewings for inmates on death row...I'd solve the problem of drunk driving by doling out shingles for the first offense, relentless sciatica for the second offense, and Ewings for the third offense. Three strikes and you are out."

Now that was economy I could understand. *God, are you paying attention?*

This wasn't the first time I had faced untimely death. Another nephew had lived only one day, and although his death was sad and his casket shockingly small, I had been able to rationalize his death. He had been born prematurely with many physical problems. I reasoned it made sense for God to take him home after so short a life. A few years ago a seventeen year old in our congregation died unexpectedly of a brain aneurysm. The shock of his death was relieved by many young folks rededicating their lives to Christ, one of whom was this nephew, now facing his own death. The teenager left behind a deeply grieving family, but he didn't leave behind a wife and two little children who **needed** him. I made sure I reminded God of this fact.

When Ethan was diagnosed I wrote his name in my Bible next to Psalm 31:15, *"My times are in thy hand..."(KJV)* Surely, surely, God agreed with me that Ethan's "time" included many, many more years. Ethan bravely endured surgery, a year of chemotherapy, and then enjoyed four months of remission and health.

Now the cancer was back. The twenty-first of December, Ethan went on hospice care in his home and bravely prepared to die. When Ethan was not well enough to attend church on Christmas Eve, our congregation took the service to him.

Ethan cheerfully greeted us from his hospital bed as we filed into the living room. His wife, Melissa, stood protectively at the head of the bed holding one year old Grant. Cassie, their three year old daughter, a bit overwhelmed by all the people, sat on Ethan's bed, eyes wide, legs draped over her dad, bare toes wiggling.

We sang of joy and hope and God's greatest gift to us. Or at least some of us sang. I couldn't. I was crying and arguing with God.

When asked if he had a request, Ethan didn't choose a Christmas carol. He asked us to sing, "Our God, He is Alive." We raised the rafters with the two part chorus, the deep manly voices leading, the higher feminine voices echoing, "There is a God, He is alive. In him we live and we survive. From dust our God created man; He is our God..." Our voices blended together for the powerful finale, "THE GREAT I AM!"

It was when we sang the third verse that God spoke to my heart.

"Secure is life from mortal mind
God holds the germ within his hand,
Though men may search, they cannot find
For God alone does understand."

God was saying to me, "My daughter, you don't have to understand. Just trust me. I hold life within my hand. I hold Ethan's life, Floyd's, and Addie's life, the confused old lady's life, your life. Your idea of fairness is not mine. Stop searching for answers, just trust me. Ethan's time is in my hand."

Watching Ethan, in the cruel clutches of cancer, join with us as we sang, "In him we live and we survive," helped me dry my tears and sing out with the group. It still made absolutely no sense, but for the moment, at least, I would trust God.

Ethan went home to be with the Lord on January 2. His first full day in heaven would have been his twenty-eighth earth birthday.

"Our God He is Alive" by A.W. Discus
Copyright 1973 Sacred Selections, used by permission.

ABOUT THE AUTHOR
Laura Hawbaker resides in Dallas Center, Iowa. She is wife of one, mom of eight, and grandma of four. She enjoys reading, writing, and taking care of her family.

To learn more about Laura go to:
http://faithwriters.com/testimonies.php

UNRAVELED

By Mimi Marie

"But God, I can't do this. I'm making a mistake. Please give me a way out!"

"Trust Me."

The unspoken dialogue between us was precise, I will never forget.

Though tears of fear and doubt poured down my face, those two simple words gave me courage to continue exchanging my wedding vows that day. Anguish replaced the joy that should've been on my heart. Because I just knew that when my husband found out who I really was, he would leave me. It wasn't a matter of if. It was a matter of when.

As I stood before God and the people who loved us, I stood broken. The eyes of the two family members who had repeatedly raped me throughout my childhood were watching. One glance from them woke the helpless, shame-based, fearful little girl. It only took their eyes for my confidence to drain dry. Within seconds, there I was, standing in a beautiful white wedding dress as a twenty-six-year-old woman, yet feeling five again.

The urge to purge reminded me that my bondage to bulimia was alive. Every restroom was mapped out in my head like a fire escape. Negative thoughts of letting everyone down wouldn't cease. They worked hard to give us a wedding—I couldn't bail. So I pretended. I pretended the same way I pretended everything was okay as a child when I really wanted to scream, "HELP!" I acted as though my tears were those of joy so I wouldn't disappoint, and I proclaimed that I truly loved the man I was marrying because I thought I was expected to. Part of me felt lucky someone wanted to marry me at all.

I spent the next four years contemplating the two simple words God had given me. Pretending to love my husband through a filter of pain left me empty; the distorted love script didn't last. I blamed him for not being patient, lying, and not living up to my expectations. I just wanted him to get it over with and leave. Eventually, our marriage ended.

Freedom from pretending was like breathing fresh mountain air. I hated to lie. But my heart remained tangled. Each knot bound to unpleasant memories and failure. Nothing I did could unravel the damage. Failing God and our children hurt. Though I prayed for forgiveness, I didn't feel forgiven, but I kept on believing.

Though I had been delivered from bulimia before our divorce and had begun my journey to heal from childhood abuse, I still had a ton of pain and sin to face. Beginning each day with God was crucial. Studying His Word, praying, and tears made our time together special. The Bible helped me distinguish truth from lies; it showed me God was in control. His hand gently unraveled one knot at a time. Lessons regarding marriage seemed irrelevant but swarmed me. Believing I would remain single until Jesus took me home, I reluctantly paid attention. God's love for me soaked in; once I received His love, I began loving myself through Him. The unworthy message I had accepted as a little girl started to vanish. Rejecting negative messages was a process. But I stayed diligent.

Meanwhile, I couldn't stand the sight of my ex-husband. Regardless that I had contributed to the break up, regret that my children had to suffer left me bitter. I wanted him to go away, but he didn't. From the children's sports events to open houses, he was there. For our boys' sake, I was glad he cared. The thing that irritated me the most was his gentleness. As edgy as I was, he treated me kindly.

After several biblically-based healing groups, God broke down walls of fear, anger, and resentment. I sought forgiveness where God led. First, I repented for doing life my way. And then He led me to my ex-husband. My flesh was stubborn. It took much prayer to get me to a place of genuine remorse. Sure, I could've written him a nice note and sent it in the mail. But God led me to personally meet with him. That morning, He revealed that the faults I accused my ex-husband of were precisely the areas He had addressed in me. Placing my expectation in Christ was vital; working out the impatience in me had been a process. I didn't hate my ex-husband, I hated me. At the foot of the cross, I wept, and repented of the sin that was in me.

We met and sat at a small table across from each other. It was awkward at first, but being obedient trumped my feeling. It had been four years since we separated, then divorced. Remorsefully, I looked into his eyes. I wasn't exactly sure what was going to happen, but I believed for the better.

"What's going on?" he asked.

"I just want to see how everything's going with you. We haven't talked in a while. Are you doing okay?" My heart sighed.

"Works busy. Still looking for a place to move to, nothing major."

As he chewed his food, I took the opportunity to build a bridge.

"I just want to apologize for hurting you." I stopped. Tears kept me from continuing.

He looked up at me. "I'm sorry too."

Focused on my sin, I cried even more. "I'm sorry for the pain I caused during our separation. I hope you can forgive me."

He answered softly, "That's okay. I know you're sorry."

"It's not okay. And I wish I could take it back."

Part of me wanted him to be angry. He wasn't.

I continued.

"But I need you to know God has healed my heart and made me whole in Him. I was unable to give you what you deserved because I was broken."

"I understand."

"I want you to tell me everything I did that hurt you."

He started to cry. "When you called me, 'Spineless,' and the way you yelled and told me you hated me. It really hurt when you went back to your old friends."

I nodded. "I'm sorry for all of that. Please forgive me."

"Of course I do. That's in the past."

Suddenly, I felt lighter. But it didn't end there.

I started to cry again. "I really wished we would have had a spiritual connection in our marriage. I really wanted that with you." Then the Holy Spirit spoke through me. "But that was not possible then, and I know that now."

He nodded.

"What would you say if we tried working things out between us?" Without warning, an unexplainable peace covered my words. Every distortion fled. A deep desire to love with my new heart took over.

Wiping his eyes he said, "I'd want nothing more than to work things out with you. I never stopped loving you."

And I believed him.

God mended everything that had unraveled in my heart due to sin. Nine days later, my husband and I were remarried.

"You, Lord, give true peace to those who depend on you, because they trust you." (Isaiah 26:3 NCV)

ABOUT THE AUTHOR

Mimi Marie is a thirty-seven-year-old wife and mother of two sons, ages eighteen and nine. She lives in the United States in La Quinta, California and enjoys writing, hiking, the beach, family time, and God's Word. She has been involved in Prison Ministry for eight years and enjoys encouraging people to trust Jesus.

Read more from Mimi: http://faithwriters.com/testimonies.php

WHY IS HE DOING THIS TO ME NOW?

By Lori Dixon

Sitting on the bench in front of the nurses' station, I was sandwiched between my eleven-year-old daughter, Mia, and my seventy-three-year-old mother, Joy. Words did not come, but we sat, three generations, silently holding hands. I glanced down, surprised at how closely my fingers resembled my mother's; Mia's were still those of a child, round and unmarred, lacking the imperfections that come from years of hard work. I held on just a little tighter to both of them . . . a love chain of over a hundred years of service to God.

Geriatrics shuffled by, lifeless eyes staring straight ahead; where they were going, I did not know. Moments later, the same menagerie appeared again, completing I surmised, an endless circle around the ward.

Feeling Mia fidget, I knew it was time to bring our visit to an end. I glanced over to the woman who looked like my mom, but whose eyes were distant, no longer reflecting the life and vitality that once brought meaning to her name.

"Well, it's time for us to get home."

Her fingers twisted harder around mine as her other hand clutched my arm. Meeting my gaze, with steely vision she looked deep into my eyes and–but for a moment–my mother reappeared.

"The Lord's been good to me my whole life . . . why is He doing this to me now?" No sooner had she finished her heartbreaking question, and she was gone again. Vague eyes looked past me, studying the empty hallway, but her hands still hung on.

I turned my eyes back to my daughter, mortified that she heard this deep, painful cry. Squeezing her little hand to give some assurance, I let go of tiny fingers and focused on my mother.

"I don't know, Mom. I just don't know." Gently, I removed her hand from my arm and gave her an awkward, one-sided hug. My words were more for me than for her as she had retreated back into her own mysterious Alzheimer's world, but the question still hung in the air.

Walking out of the lodge that day, I was not the same person. A shift had occurred between the Lord and me. Anger began to grow, its roots burying deeper and deeper into my soul. Strangling tendrils tightened around my heart, choking my faith.

She had been so faithful to Him.

Why did He do this to her?

What kind of God did I serve?

As the months went by, I wrestled with what would be the last coherent, articulated sentence I would ever hear my mother say. A woman of strong faith her whole life, a godly example of trusting the Lord ... and then she drops this bomb. Shrapnel ripped into my heart, internal bleeding seeping into every crevice of my being as I attempted to continue to stumble through life ... a silent walking wounded.

Why God? Why?

The visits to the lodge became harder and harder for me—her question echoed in my mind each time I saw her. I would stay up late at night, sending out random emails to any man of faith I could find online: priests, protestant pastors, rabbis. I just kept searching for the answer to my Mother's question. It was a crazy quest to fill the void before she passed away. My faith was waning as I ran farther and farther from God with each email response. No man of God could give a satisfying answer. No book on any shelf could either. I would spend hours in countless devotions and in the Word, but it was all white noise as nothing could be heard over the drum of the unanswered question.

Life was becoming empty and meaningless.

With each passing season, the root of anger burrowed down.

My mother's last days were peaceful, and she passed after her seventy-fifth birthday and just before my forty-fourth. Since I was the only girl and a writer, my brothers asked me to give the eulogy. It would appear I had even fooled them; they had no idea of the pain and resentment planted in my heart.

The night before the funeral, I sat in the dark; a word count of zero mocked me from my laptop.

What could I say? All I could think of–all I had thought of–was the monstrous unanswered question.

A dark shadow appeared at the top of the basement stairs; it was my brother who was staying with me from out of town. "How's it going?"

That was all he had to say. A flood gate opened as I confessed my anger and shared our mom's last statement.

"Oh, wow," he said without pause, filling his glass of water, "that's easy."

That's easy?

"What do you mean, 'That's easy?' It's so not easy. I've asked everyone, and so far, not one decent answer."

He plopped down onto the couch next to me, rubbing his eyes. "You never asked me." With a crooked, pained grin he continued, "You know it's kind of like when parents drop off their kids for Sunday school; some of them can just pass their children over the gate, give them a kiss, and then leave. But others have to come inside, sit next to their little ones, and play until they are distracted; then they scoot out unnoticed. Well, God knew how much we needed Mom, how much we ran to her for advice, and how she was so much a part of our walk of faith. If He had taken her in her sleep or with a heart attack, we couldn't have handled the shock. We needed her too much.

"Instead, out of grace, He allowed her to sit with us, and colour for a bit. He let her sneak out of our lives slowly so that we could adjust and learn to walk with Him on our own. He loves Mom, and all of us, that much." Patting my knee, he took his water and headed for the stairs. "I'm so sorry you've struggled with that. I've known

154

it all along; it's how I've had peace. I wish you would have asked me sooner."

Watching his back disappear down the stairs, the bright light from the blank, stark Word document was burning my eyes. Or perhaps it was the tears.

Finally, I could write my goodbye; or rather my 'see ya later, Mom.' I had found the answer we were looking for; the question that had made me doubt my own faith.

The Lord had been good to my mother her whole life … and, with amazing love and grace, continued to be good until the very end. So faithful, He gave the answer just in time for me to share it with passion and newfound faith to all those who came to celebrate my mother's life—with JOY!

ABOUT THE AUTHOR

Lori Dixon is an award-winning, Canadian writer and speaker with over 200 articles published, many of which are archived in the National Library of Canada. Her passion is bringing truth to women, speaking in love, and seeing lives transformed through the power of the Word. She does so in humorous ways, using props, practical applications, and more often than not, expository teaching.

Follow her ramblings which vary from humorous to hard-hitting at http://faithwriters.com/testimonies.php .

TRIALS AND TRIUMPHS

A TESTIMONY
THAT INSPIRED ME

A MAN CALLED HARRY

By Jim Oates

The first time I met Harry was in the early 1990s. He was a tall gangly man who looked to be in his mid-fifties, but it is hard to tell the age of a person in Harry's condition. He could not walk without the aid of a wheeled walker, and his spindly legs wobbled as he made his way to the activity room where we held our weekly Bible study.

Along with my friend Don, I had been conducting Bible studies at a local nursing home facility for several years. While rounding up residents for our meeting on this particular Sunday morning, I went to the sitting room at the other end of the building where I found a few of our regulars watching TV. I asked Mrs. O'Keeffe, "Would you like to come to Bible study this morning?"

The fine looking lady, always dressed to the nines, nodded her head.

I said, "I'd be happy to help with your wheelchair." As I busied myself with the task, I noticed a poorly dressed man with spittle dribbling from his chin onto the front of his shirt sitting near her, waving his hand uncontrollably in the air. He was new to the home, and I had never seen him before. He wasn't what I would call a handsome man, but he might have been if he had a little more flesh on his bones.

Harry couldn't speak other than a few unrecognizable utterances like, "Ahhhh ahhhh, ah ah," but this didn't deter him from trying to communicate. After my invitation, he grasped his walker and stood to his unsteady legs. With his boney finger waggling at me and that, "Ahhhh ahhhh, ah ah," I instinctively knew he wanted to come.

Inside I cringed and then said, "We're holding a service down

159

the hall in the activity room." All the while, I was hoping and praying that he wouldn't come. I didn't want him there. *He'll make funny noises and distract the service. I've seen people like him before. They always gurgle and grunt while and doing weird things. He'd be an embarrassment.*

As I was pushing Mrs. O'Keeffe along, Harry passed us, weaving his way down the long corridor. This godly man that I thought I was, bringing the word of God to these shut-ins, was thoroughly embarrassed.

Yes, Harry did come, and he did make funny noises, he always sat over against the wall in the front row He seemed to enjoy the songs that were sung, and appeared to listen intently to every word that was said. I was still embarrassed, but noticed every time the name of Jesus or God was said, Harry's hand shot up with that boney finger waggling heavenward while saying, loud enough for everyone to hear, "Ahhhh ahhhh, ah ah." Of course, all eyes turned to Harry on these occasions, and a chorus of, "Shush, shh," were said all around the room which were actually more distracting than Harry. This went on for several weeks.

One morning, under the leading of the Holy Spirit, I took a side trip from my prepared study. "God loves each one of us, no matter our status in life, our family background, or education. None of this matters to God. He loves each and every one of us the same."

I went on to say, "Maybe as a child, other kids made fun of you. Maybe someone said that you would never amount to anything. God loves you too much to say anything like that because He really values you. It doesn't matter what other people say about you. God cares, and has made a way for you to draw near to Him, and to feel His comforting arms around you. He did this by bringing His Son, Jesus, to this earth to die for each and every person."

Not thinking of any particular person, I went on to say, "Maybe your parents may even have said, 'You are stupid! You're no good; you will never amount to anything.'" At that moment, Harry got to his feet and weaved his way across the floor. He stood directly in front of me, about a foot away. He was staring intently into my eyes, and with that boney finger thumping against his chest, he said, "Ahhhh, ahhhh, ah, ah."

Taken aback, I said, "You Harry? They said that to you?"

Harry replied with that same thumping of his chest all the while saying, "Ahhhh, ahhhh, ah, ah."

My superior status crumbled right then and there. The Holy Spirit spoke directly to me. I didn't hear His voice; Harry did the speaking for Him.

I repented right there, and prayed silently. *Dear Jesus, Please forgive me for looking at one of your loved ones as a lesser being than myself. Please prevent me from ever judging others by their outward appearances again. In Jesus' name I pray. Amen.*

I saw Harry in a totally new light after that, and grew to love him. I looked forward to seeing him every Sunday morning. I took delight in watching him praise God, with that boney finger reaching heavenward, and hearing that familiar, "Ahhhh, ahhhh, ah, ah."

Harry continued coming to our Bible study for several months. One morning, the nurse announced, "Harry died last night."

I have no doubt that Harry is now in Glory with his beloved Jesus. My colleague Don and I often spoke of Harry, and we rejoiced that Harry was finally free. There was so much he wanted to say, so much he wanted to do, and now he is released from the prison of the disease-racked body that held him captive all those years. We often wondered what Harry might be doing in Heaven. We pictured him running through fields of flowers shouting and singing at the top of his voice, but no more "Ahhh, ahhhh, ah, ah's."

I thank God for speaking to me through this man who suffered from that horrible disease. I learned a valuable lesson that day and believe I am a better person today because of a man called Harry.

ABOUT THE AUTHOR

Jim Oates lives in Essex, Ontario, Canada where he teaches a Bible Class at a local senior residence. He has written the biography of his late wife, *Wilma a Lady of Courage and Dignity*, as well as several short stories and has had some published. He is now working on his memoirs, which he's calling *Hodgepodge*.

To read more of his work, go to:
http://faithwriters.com/testimonies.php

A TIME BOMB IN MY TUMMY ANNE'S STORY

By Luella Campbell

On 24 April 1970, my son, Andrew, was born, but what should have been a mother's most joyous occasion turned into a very long nightmare.

During my stay in the maternity hospital, and unbeknown to me, I was given more than an immunisation during a measles scare. I was the unwitting recipient of a ticking time bomb via a "dirty" needle. But this was a secret invader as no one knew it was there.

Three months after Andrew's birth, I came down with a severe case of what was diagnosed as hepatitis. After my recovery, I was never quite well, nothing specific, but at the same time I was neither really sick nor well. I ignored it and carried on with my hectic and eventful life as a wife and mother in the ever-changing, political upheaval of Zimbabwe.

About twelve years after I contracted the "bomb," and still ignorant of its evil presence in my liver, my legs began to swell. By this time, we had moved to Maseru in Lesotho where, after a famine of luxuries in Zimbabwe, we bought nuts. With great delight, I feasted on almonds and paid the price–a severe bout of vomiting which lasted the whole night. My ailing liver could not cope with the unexpected bounty.

After a tough eighteen months in Maseru, we thankfully relocated to Alice, a small town in one of the, then, black homelands of South Africa, the Ciskei. My husband worked for a Christian organization called ACAT (Africa Co-operation Action Trust), and I helped him as his secretary and "girl Friday." Miracles were our way of life. God was always one step ahead, smoothing the way and providing for us in one nail-biting episode after another.

After six years in ACAT, we moved to Stutterheim, a small town in the Eastern Cape where we lived for seven years. These were years of more severe testing than we had ever experienced in our Christian walk. Betrayal by a fellow believer in a business venture and my deteriorating health left us penniless and cast totally on the mercy and faithfulness of our God. I went into liver failure, gained forty pounds of fluid in my body, almost overnight, and spent six days in an East London hospital in a coma. The diagnosis was cirrhosis of the liver, but from what? The time bomb was still ticking and coming perilously close to the end of the fuse. I was bedridden for five months. One day, desperately ill and alone at home, I received a phone call from my doctor. He informed me of the shocking news that, without a liver transplant, I would die. I cried out to God, *"What now?"*

God heard my heart and comforted me with the words of Psalm 118:17, *"I will not die but live, and will proclaim what the Lord has done."(NIV)* My fear gave way to a peaceful trust which never left me through the many months of my trial.

There were obstacles to negotiate over the next few months, medical aid approval, someone to take care of my husband and daughter (by this time my son was in college), accommodation for my family in Cape Town where I was to have the transplant and, by no means least, a donor type B liver small enough to fit me. I was flown to Groote Schuur Hospital in November 1990 where the doctor realised that my physical condition was too bad for an immediate transplant.

I asked the Lord for a liver for Christmas. On 17 December 1990, after an eleven-hour operation, my prayer was granted. In God's mercy, although I failed all the conditions for a transplant and had only three days to live, I received the liver of a twenty-year old Basuto lad who, after a car accident, had died in Victoria Hospital, Wynberg, Cape.

The operation itself was not without its miracles. At the critical moment when the blood vessels of the donor liver were being attached, I began to bleed. After forty-eight units of blood, when the surgeons were at the point of pulling the sheet over me, the bleeding stopped and they were able to attach the new liver successfully. They could not explain why they had persevered, but I could. It was God, fulfilling His promise to me!

After my transplant, my shrivelled up, hard, non-functioning liver was sent to London where the "bomb" was finally identified–hepatitis B. The astute physician, Dr Wendy Spearman, head of the Liver Transplant Unit at Groote Schuur Hospital, traced the whole saga back to the measles vaccine I had received after Andrew's birth.

My recovery was slow and painful, a month in the hospital, and then blood tests twice a week and three-times-a-day temperature checks after my discharge. After three months in Cape Town, I was finally on my way home. I still had a long battle to face: the necessary precautionary semi-isolation, the indignity of having to wear a mask in the company of people other than my immediate family, the migraines, and inevitable depression that followed my long battle with death, but...God was there.

And now? After my transplant, I was assured of at least another five years of life and yet, here I am, more than twenty years later, still living in the FOG (favour of God)! A new liver was never the guarantee of a trouble-free life. The virus is still alive in my adopted liver, but kept at bay by anti-retroviral drugs which bring with them their own set of problems, as have the anti-rejection drugs which are as necessary as my daily food. Cortisone has destroyed my bones, leaving behind a trail of spontaneous fractures and all the pain associated with broken bones. My kidneys always teeter on the edge of malfunction with the daily load of drugs they have to process. I am monitored constantly for the bodily functions that tell me I am still alive.

So many amazing evidences of God's love and mercy surface as I reflect on my eventful life–times without number when God was one step ahead, smoothing the bumpy path for me, family members who loved, supported and cared for me when I was helpless and bedridden, friends who "happened" to be in the right place at the right time when I needed help, a shoulder to cry on, a word from God's Word to encourage me, or someone to transport the children, do the cooking, washing and ironing, or just to "be there."

Through it all I have discovered that God's love is absolutely amazing!

ABOUT THE AUTHOR

Luella Annette Campbell is a seventy-three year old, Pastoral Assistant at Ebenezer Family Church, King William's Town, South Africa. She is a retired trained nurse, mother of four married sons, grandmother of seven grandsons and one granddaughter. She teaches three discipleship classes at her church, writes teaching material for use in the Home Cells, and magazine articles for her church magazine. She posts daily articles on two websites, and is in the process of publishing Scripture textbooks for Christian and Catholic schools in India for Grades one to eight.

Read more from Luella:
http://faithwriters.com/testimonies.php

HE CAME TO STAY IN MY HEART

By Pauline Brakebill

He came to stay
One bright and sunny day.
Into our hearts, he found a way
Of warming that piece of clay.

He was born so many years ago.
His mind, they said, would never grow.
But who of us would ever know
The joy, laughter, and wisdom he would bestow?

His name, John Patrick Murphy,
An Irishman, who claimed the trophy
Of hair so red and eyes so blue.
A temper to match, through and through.

His birth mother and dad, with reason,
Loaned him to us for a season.
To twelve brothers and sisters he brought
The patience, love, and laughter they sought.

His memory put us aghast
Of tales and happenings in the past.
Just ask him, he'd know, he'd remember
Events each year from January to December.

Open and honest was John.
No, not one, did he come upon
Who left without a word of friendship.
Kisses came freely and genuinely from his lips.

Work, for John, was such a joy
With money to earn for that dear boy,
Taking family and friends to dinner
With hard-earned pay was such a winner.

He came to stay.
God had a plan; it was His way
To touch the hearts of many a soul.
John was His messenger, so pure and whole.

John loved the Lord.
So by example, his heart he poured
To all he met, their souls to save.
His Heavenly crown with many stars, he'll have.

There were several friends,
John felt his mission not complete
Until he saw them safe and
Secured for Heaven's street.

John loved to sing
Praises to God, his Savior and King.
His voice, though flawed, surely would ring
In the courts of the Lord, a sweet savor it did bring.

Now he has gone to stay
In that Holy City for ever and a day.
Never more to suffer or cry,
Looking at God's Glory from on high.

He will be waiting for those
Who, on that day, did choose
To receive Christ as their Savior.
They too, like John, will go to stay!

HALLELUJAH!!

ABOUT THE AUTHOR

Pauline Brakebill lives with her husband, Quintin, of fifty-six years in the Beautiful Ozark Mountains in northern Arkansas. She has six children, twenty-two grandchildren, and one great grand-child, with another one on the way. She has been writing all of her life. In the last twenty years, Pauline has explored many different genres. She thanks God for putting up with her all of these many years.

John was the first Brakebill family's foster child. He came to them in 1972 at the age of four, and remained with the family until he died of cancer at the age of thirty-one in 1998. John was such a blessing to all he who knew him. The love of the Lord was in his heart, and that love shone to all who came in contact with John.

To read more of Pauline's work, go to:
http://faithwriters.com/testimonies.php

EPILOGUE

There's an interesting introduction Christians often overlook in the opening sentences of Matthew chapter four. Immediately, the reader is introduced to three key players: Jesus, the Spirit, and the devil. It is thought-provoking to notice who is leading Jesus to be tempted by the devil—namely, the Spirit. Matthew goes on to say, *"after fasting forty days and forty nights, He was hungry."* (Matthew 4:2 ESV) Succinctly put, the Holy Spirit led a hungry, *very hungry*, Jesus, directly to the location of Satan for the specific purpose of tempting.

Of course, Christ's resolve was powerful enough to reject the devil's enticements, but not without suffering. In Christ's humanity, He had built supernatural muscles. In order to produce muscles, even small ones, trauma to the muscle fibers must be executed. When the fibers repair themselves, they overcompensate to form larger muscles each time they're damaged. Although the science of understanding how muscles form is complex, one thing is clear even to the most uneducated layman—the only way to cause trauma to a muscle fiber is by resistance. And this "resisting" must be repeated over a short period of time. As if that isn't torturous enough, to make muscles grow larger, it isn't enough to continue lifting/pushing/pulling the same amount of weight you started with, the resistance must grow weightier.

The Spirit knew that even a forty-day-fasted Christ could handle the weighty resistance of Satan's temptations to turn stones into bread. Thankfully, Christians aren't usually given such heavy loads, especially in the infant stages of conversion, lest the weight of it would crush us. Nevertheless, believers are called to be Christ-followers, even, and *especially*, when the path leads into a wilderness of temptation. There is no other way, no short cut, no exemption for building spiritual muscles—the trauma must occur.

It's only the victor, Jesus Christ, who gives people a way to experience a triumphant life, a powerful and durable journey. Through Christ, we are built up, made strong, and through Him, suffering and heartache have eternal purposes. Christianity is not for the weak-willed or temporal-minded. Only those who, as instructed in Matthew 6:33 (ESV), continue to *seek first the kingdom of God and His righteousness,* will persevere—because these are the things worthy of trauma, and the muscles built on this training field will last forever.

Now, in all these things we are more than conquerors through him who loved us. For I am sure that neither death nor life, nor angels nor rulers, nor things present nor things to come, nor powers, nor height nor depth, nor anything else in all creation, will be able to separate us from the love of God in Christ Jesus our Lord. (Romans 8:37-39 ESV)

Paula Titus

INVITATION TO ACCEPT JESUS

In our confusing world where feelings often trump truth, we want to make it crystal clear why everyone needs Jesus. It's not to solve your problems, make you wealthy, or heal your sickness. As a matter of fact, your problems may get worse, at least temporarily. Everyone needs Jesus because He is our only way to righteousness. Righteousness is a sort of "rightness." With Christ we can be "right" with humanity, with our own conscience, with God. To be right with God means He has forgiven us and made us His own children. To be right with humanity means we learn to love others, put others before ourselves, and live in humility. To be right with our own conscience means we can sleep soundly at night, and in the morning, when we look in the mirror, we don't have to feel ashamed of our past mistakes because we know God the Father so lovingly put them to death when He nailed them to the cross of Christ. Everyone needs Jesus because without Him, everything—your relationship to God, relationships with others, even how you view yourself—is all wrong, askew, and perverse. There is forgiveness in Jesus alone, righteousness in Him alone, everlasting life in Him alone. Come to Christ and you may find yourself in the center of a fearsome hurricane like so many of the writers in this book; the winds of life whipping and screaming all around. But when you know the wind is in the sovereign hands of the One who has called you His child, it suddenly isn't so frightening after all.

"Dear Lord Jesus,
I know I am a sinner, and I ask for your forgiveness. I
believe you died for my sins and rose from the dead. I
trust and follow you as my Lord and Savior. Guide my
life and help me to do your will.
In your name, amen."